SUN, STARS & PLANETS

By Tom Stacy
Illustrated by Peter Bull
& Sebastian Quigley

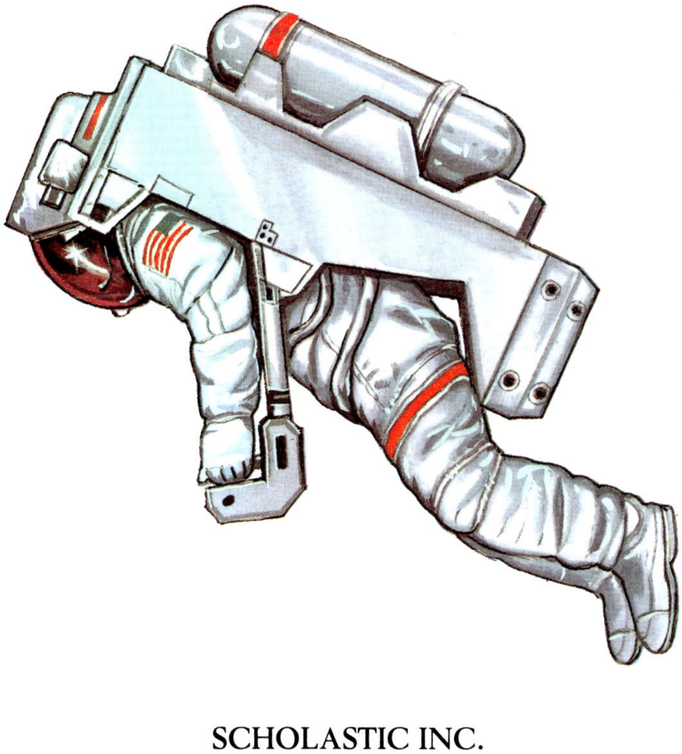

SCHOLASTIC INC.
New York Toronto London Auckland Sydney

Contents

 Originally published in Great Britain by Kingfisher Books, a Grisewood & Dempsey Company. This edition is published by Scholastic Inc., 730 Broadway, New York, NY 10003, by arrangement with Random House, Inc.
Printed in the U.S.A.
ISBN 0-590-45979-1

5 6 7 8 9 10 08 99 98 97 96

What is the sun like?

The sun is a star, one of the billions in space. It is like a giant powerhouse – a glowing ball of hot gases, producing a vast amount of energy which streams out through space in waves of light and heat. This energy is essential to life on Earth. Without it our planet would be too cold and dark for plants and animals to survive.

NEVER LOOK AT THE SUN

The sun is far too bright for our eyes. Never look directly at it, even when wearing sunglasses. Its rays are strong enough to damage your eyes or even to cause blindness.

SUN FACTS

- The sun is about 93 million miles from Earth.
- It is about 4.6 billion years old.
- It spins around once every 27.4 days.
- It is an average star. Some stars are thousands of times brighter, others are thousands of times fainter.
- The sun's diameter is nearly 865,400 miles – 109 times Earth's. One million Earths could fit inside the sun!

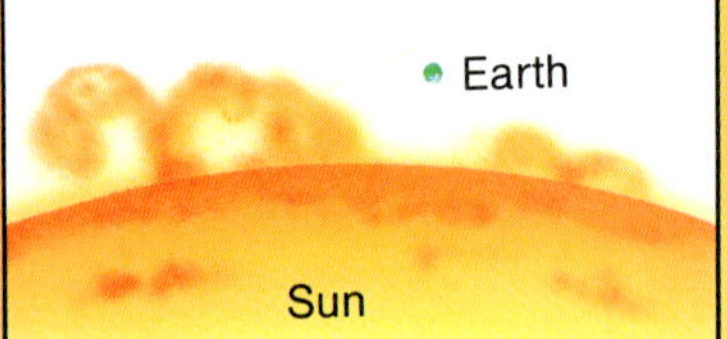

Around the sun is a layer of gas called the chromosphere. It stretches out into space for about 6,200 miles.

Plumes of hot gas called prominences shoot thousands of miles into space. Some last for hours, others for days.

Sunspots are cooler areas which look like dark blotches on the sun's surface. They are most common about every 11 years.

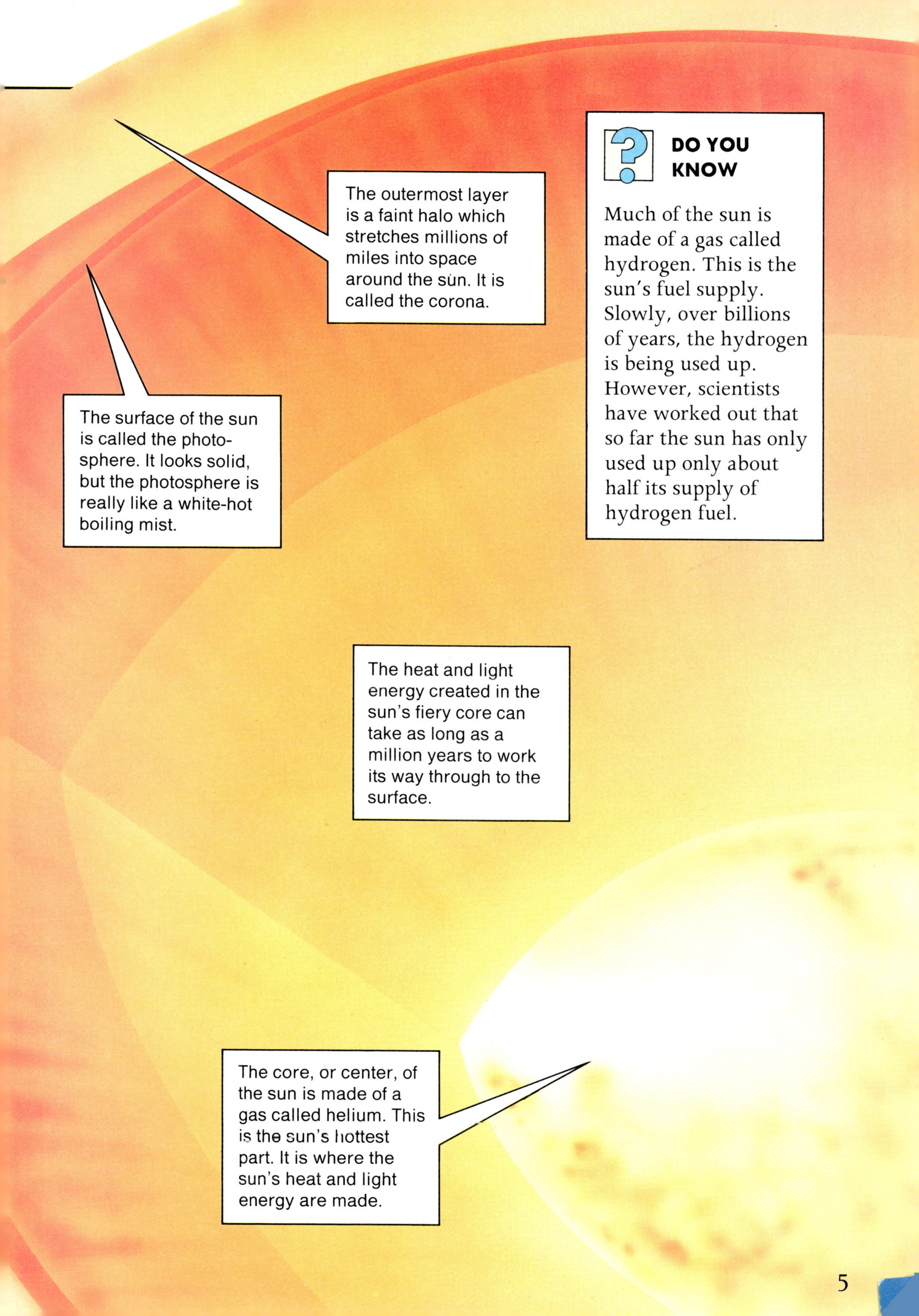

DO YOU KNOW

Much of the sun is made of a gas called hydrogen. This is the sun's fuel supply. Slowly, over billions of years, the hydrogen is being used up. However, scientists have worked out that so far the sun has only used up only about half its supply of hydrogen fuel.

How hot is the sun?

The sun is far too hot to visit! The hottest part is the core, where the temperature can reach 27 million°F. Even the coolest part of the sun, its surface, is 10,800°F – at this temperature solid iron would boil away into clouds of gas! All this heat is made in the sun's fiery core by a process in which hydrogen gas is changed into another gas, called helium.

DO YOU KNOW

The sun is always losing weight! In fact, scientists have worked out that it loses around $4\frac{1}{2}$ million tons every second – this is the amount of hydrogen gas that the sun turns into energy every second.

DO YOU KNOW

All substances are made of tiny, invisible atoms, which have huge amounts of energy. Some of this energy is given out inside the sun, where it is so hot that hydrogen atoms break up, joining together again to form helium atoms. This is called an atomic reaction.

MAKE A SUNDIAL

Push a stick into modeling clay and stand it on a sheet of paper in a sunny place. Use a ruler and a pencil to mark on the paper the places where the shadow falls at different times of the day.

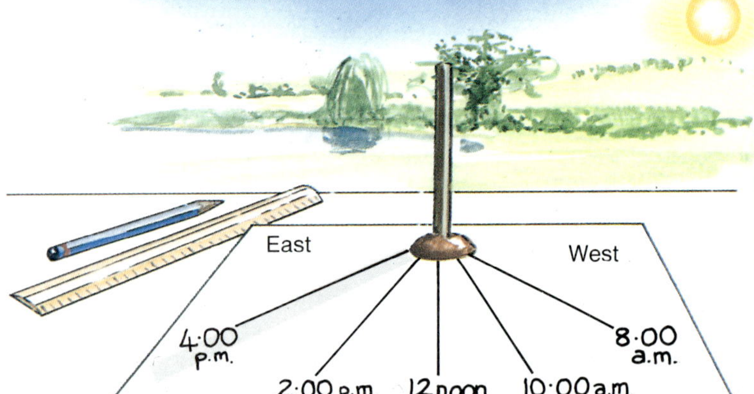

Why does the sun rise?

Although we can't feel it, Earth is always moving. It orbits, or goes around, the sun, and this journey takes a year. At the same time, Earth itself is spinning – one complete spin every 24 hours. As Earth spins, the sun comes into view and seems to us to rise in the sky. Earth spins from west to east, so the sun is in the east when we first see it in the morning, and in the west when it sets in the evening.

DO YOU KNOW

Although we can't feel it, Earth spins at 994 miles per hour (mph). The central line on which something spins is called an axis. Earth's axis passes through the North and South Poles.

How old is the sun?

The sun is around 4.6 billion years old. Stars are like people – they are born, live for a while, and finally die. Our sun is an average star in size and brightness. It has now reached middle age, but in another 5 billion years or so it will have used up all its hydrogen fuel. Then it will swell to as much as 100 times its present size and become a red giant. After millions more years, this giant sun will shrink and become a white dwarf. As it cools down, it will stop shining altogether.

DO YOU KNOW

Light bulbs cool in much the same way as dying stars do – the filament, or wire, inside glows white, then yellow, orange, and finally red.

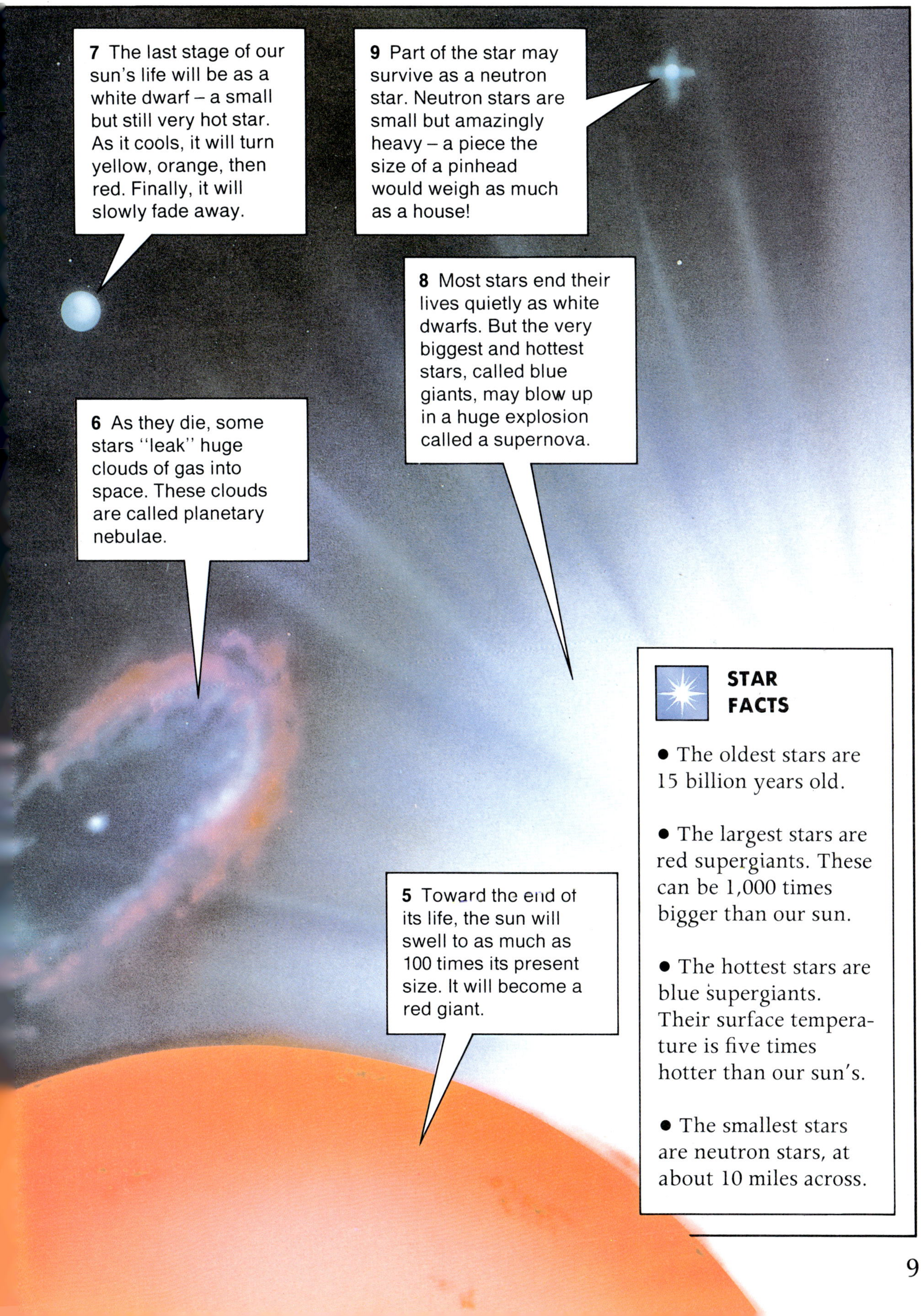

5 Toward the end of its life, the sun will swell to as much as 100 times its present size. It will become a red giant.

6 As they die, some stars "leak" huge clouds of gas into space. These clouds are called planetary nebulae.

7 The last stage of our sun's life will be as a white dwarf – a small but still very hot star. As it cools, it will turn yellow, orange, then red. Finally, it will slowly fade away.

8 Most stars end their lives quietly as white dwarfs. But the very biggest and hottest stars, called blue giants, may blow up in a huge explosion called a supernova.

9 Part of the star may survive as a neutron star. Neutron stars are small but amazingly heavy – a piece the size of a pinhead would weigh as much as a house!

STAR FACTS

- The oldest stars are 15 billion years old.
- The largest stars are red supergiants. These can be 1,000 times bigger than our sun.
- The hottest stars are blue supergiants. Their surface temperature is five times hotter than our sun's.
- The smallest stars are neutron stars, at about 10 miles across.

What is a black hole?

Black holes are the remains of collapsed stars. A tug of war is going on inside every star. On one side is the star's gravity, or pulling force, which is trying to make it collapse and become much smaller. On the other side is the energy pouring out from the star's core, which is trying to make it explode. For most of a star's life, its gravity and its energy balance exactly. But when the star's core runs out of fuel, gravity wins and the star collapses. The gravity around the star is now so strong that even its own light is sucked in, making it invisible – a black hole in space.

DO YOU KNOW

If the sun ever becomes a black hole, its diameter will shrink from nearly 865,400 miles to less than 4 miles.

This picture shows what would happen if a black hole and a star were close in space – the black hole's gravity would suck in hot gases from the star.

What are shooting stars?

Shooting stars, or meteors, are the streaks of light you sometimes see at night. They are made by pea-sized bits of rock or metal called meteoroids, which fall from space and burn up in Earth's atmosphere.

DO YOU KNOW

Meteoroids which fall to Earth are called meteorites. The largest meteorite on record weighs about 66 tons and measures roughly 9 feet by 8 feet.

Large meteoroids sometimes survive to fall to Earth. One that fell in Arizona left a crater which is 575 feet deep.

MAKING CRATERS

1 Fill a tray or box with damp sand, at least 4 inches deep. Drop a marble or a pebble into the sand. Does the hole look anything like the Arizona crater shown above?

2 Try dropping larger pebbles from higher up.

The bigger the pebble, and the farther it falls, the deeper the crater – the same thing happens when meteoroids fall to Earth from space.

What is Halley's comet?

Comets are huge clouds of gas and dust, much bigger than Earth, with a rocky core a few miles across. Halley's comet is named after the English scientist Edmond Halley (1656–1742), who worked out that the comet's orbit around the sun brings it close to Earth every 76 years.

DO YOU KNOW

Halley's comet was last seen in 1985–86 and will return in 2061–62. The same comet has been seen regularly since 240 BC. It appeared in 1066 at the time of the Norman Conquest of England – it is shown as a fiery star on a scene in the Bayeux tapestry, a famous strip of cloth, which tells the story of the conquest.

Why do stars twinkle?

It is Earth's atmosphere that makes stars twinkle. On its way to Earth, starlight passes through bands of warm and cold air in the atmosphere. These bands, or heat currents, make the starlight flicker. You can see the same effect if you look at distant lights through the heat currents above a bonfire.

DO YOU KNOW

Stars are always in the sky, even though they seem to disappear by day. Our star, the sun, makes the daytime sky too bright for light from other stars to show up.

STAR COMPASS

If you are in the Northern Hemisphere, look for the star group called the Big Dipper. Two of its stars point to the North Star – face it to look north. In the Southern Hemisphere, find the brightest star in the Southern Cross. Imagine a line in the sky four times as long as its longest part. Face the point at the end of this line to look to the south.

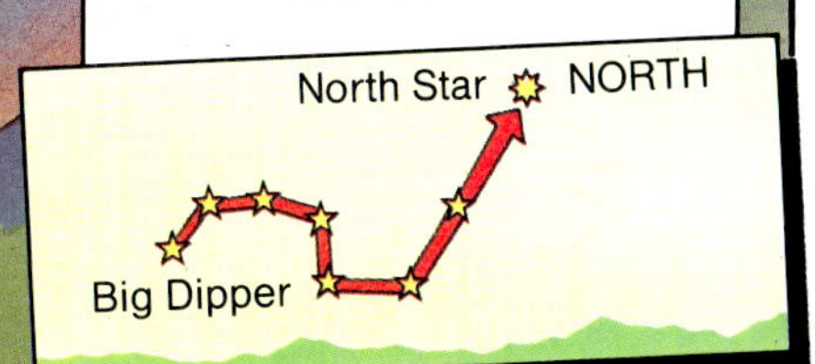

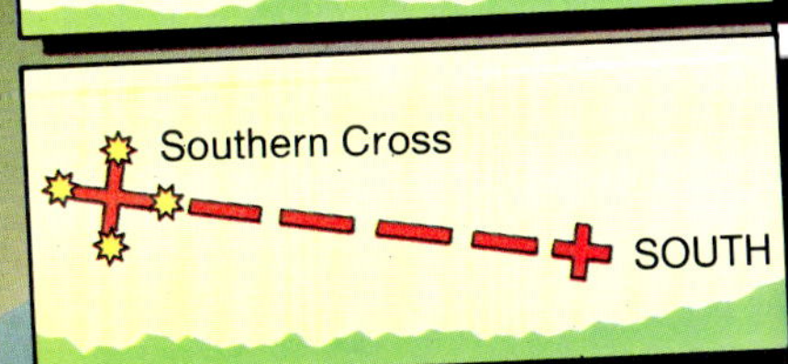

What are the signs of the zodiac?

The signs of the zodiac are 12 constellations – groups of stars which make patterns in the night sky. These 12 constellations form a ring around the sky, and the planets are always somewhere in this ring. If we could see the stars in daytime, we would see that the sun appears to move right around the zodiac in one year, spending a month or so crossing each constellation.

CONSTELLATION FACTS

- In all, 88 constellations have now been named. About half of them can be seen on any clear night. Some, such as the Great Bear, are very large. Others, such as Crux — the Cross — are very small.
- Many constellations, including those in the zodiac, were named long ago, after animals and ancient gods and heroes.
- Although from Earth they seem to be in a group, individual stars in a constellation may be huge distances apart. Some are much farther from Earth than others.

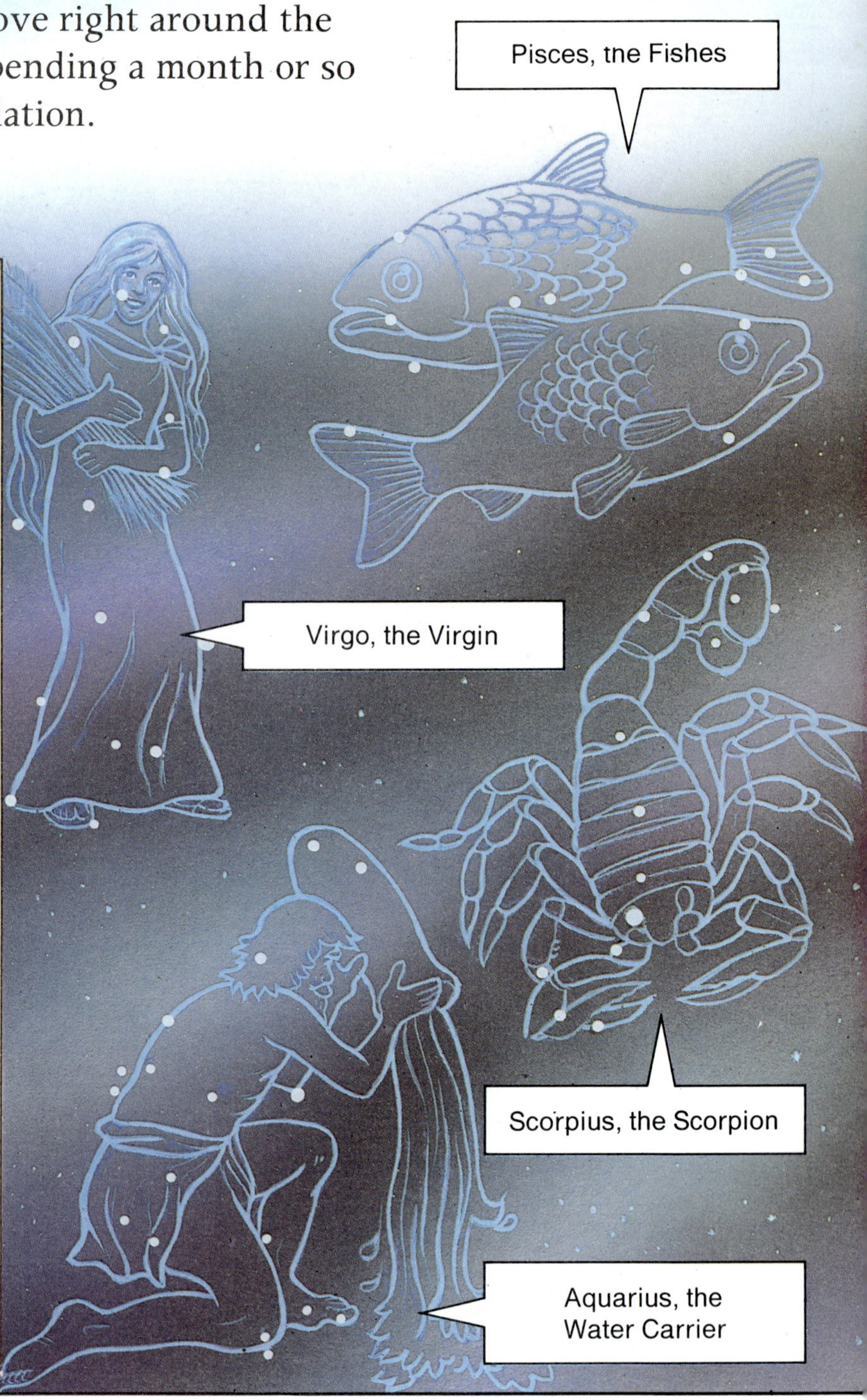

Sagittarius, the Archer
Taurus, the Bull
Aries, the Ram
Leo, the Lion
Libra, the Balance
Gemini, the Twins
Cancer, the Crab
Capricornus, the Goat

What do astronomers do?

Astronomers are scientists who study the stars. Before the telescope was invented in the 1600s, astronomers had to rely on their eyes alone. With the telescope, they could see much farther into space, and they discovered other planets and millions more stars. Today, astronomers also have radio telescopes, which they use to study invisible types of energy given off by distant stars and planets.

DO YOU KNOW

Not counting our sun, the star nearest to us is Proxima Centauri. Its light takes four years to reach us. Even if we could travel to this star, the journey would take a very long time – as you can see!

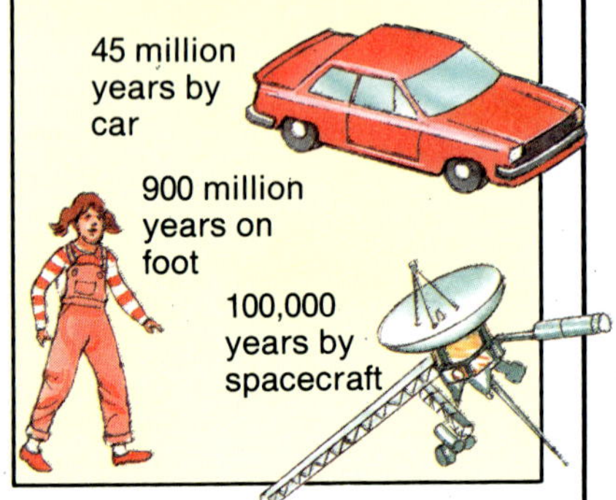

Some satellites study x-rays from space. The satellites orbit Earth outside the atmosphere, which stops the dangerous x-rays from reaching the ground.

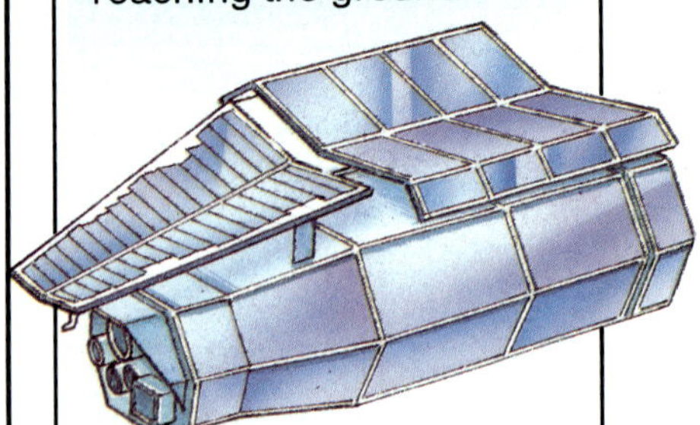

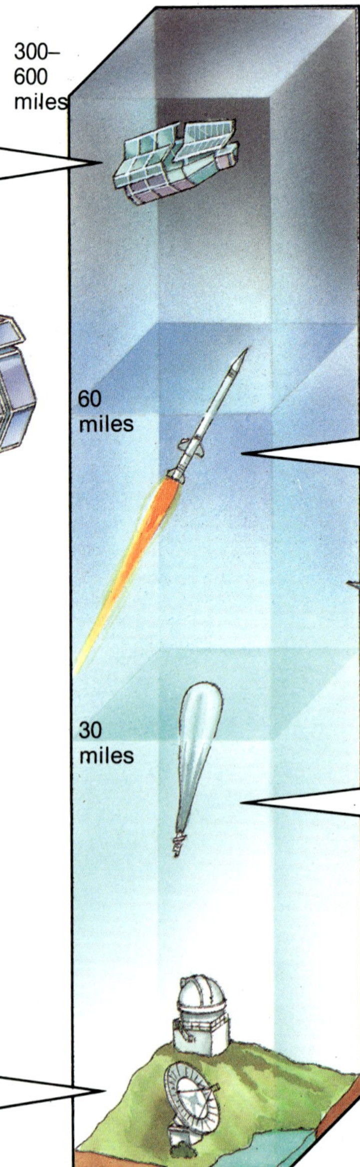

Rockets fired into the upper atmosphere send information back to Earth by parachute.

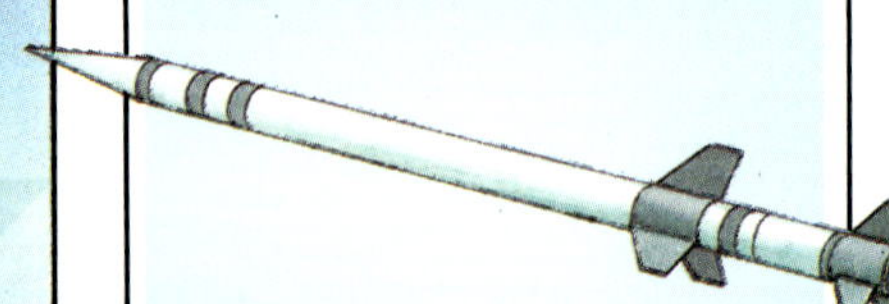

Giant telescopes collect light from space. Most are in observatories on mountain peaks. Satellite dishes pick up radio waves from space.

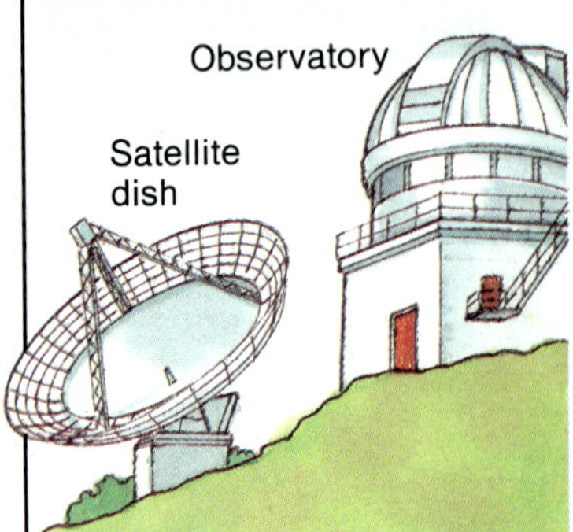

Large balloons carry experiments and measuring equipment high into the sky. They are much cheaper than rockets or satellites. The balloons are controlled from ground stations.

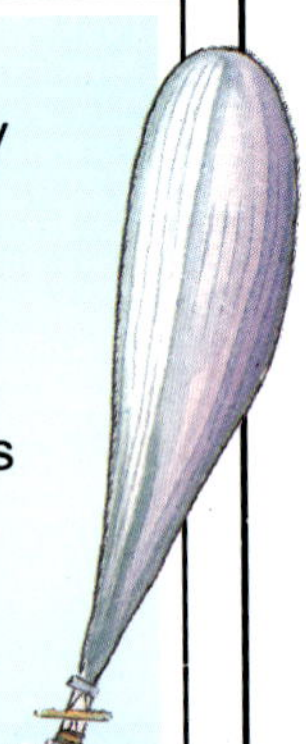

What is a satellite?

A satellite is something that orbits a planet. Until the space age began, Earth's only satellite was the moon. Now Earth also has many artificial satellites – machines which orbit the planet, doing all kinds of jobs. Some satellites relay TV and telephone signals. Some study the stars, others study Earth and its weather.

DO YOU KNOW

To escape Earth's gravity and go into orbit, a satellite must be boosted by a rocket to a speed of over 17,000 mph. The first satellite, Sputnik 1, was sent up in 1957. It lasted 92 days.

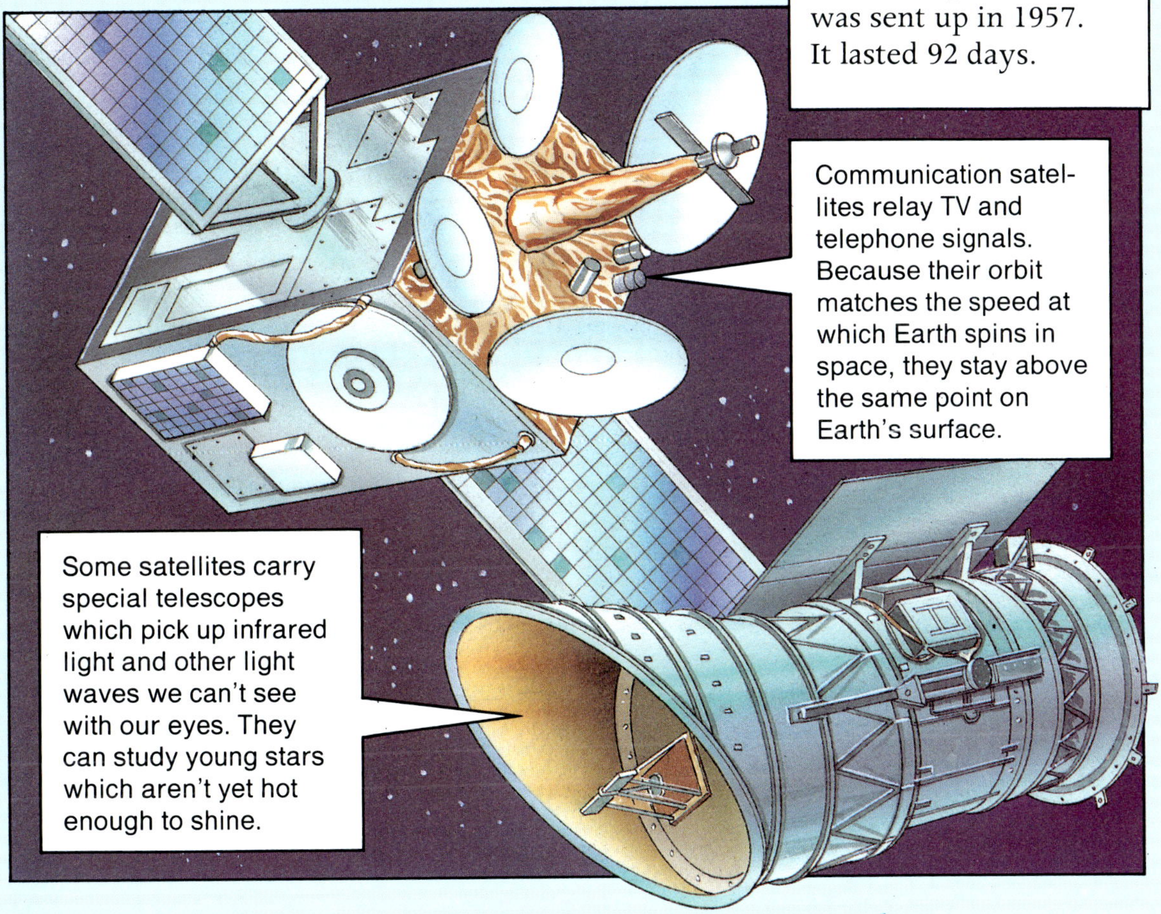

Communication satellites relay TV and telephone signals. Because their orbit matches the speed at which Earth spins in space, they stay above the same point on Earth's surface.

Some satellites carry special telescopes which pick up infrared light and other light waves we can't see with our eyes. They can study young stars which aren't yet hot enough to shine.

Satellites send information down to Earth as radio signals. These are received by satellite dishes at ground stations in different parts of the world.

What is the Milky Way?

On clear, moonless nights you may have seen a fuzzy band of starlight in the sky – this is the Milky Way. It is the huge group of stars to which our sun belongs. Star groups like the Milky Way are called galaxies, and there are millions of them in space. The Milky Way is a spiral-shaped galaxy – the picture here shows what it looks like from above. From the side it would look like a flat spinning dish.

GALAXY FACTS

- The Milky Way is made up of over 100 billion stars. The sun is just one of them.
- From edge to edge, the Milky Way is about 100,000 light-years across.
- The galaxy nearest to our own is 150,000 light-years away. It is called the Large Magellanic Cloud, and it is smaller than the Milky Way.
- There are three main kinds of galaxies. Some are spiral-shaped, like the Milky Way. Others are elliptical (egg-shaped) or irregular (uneven).

STAR GAZING

On a clear, dark night, you can see lots of stars without the help of binoculars or a telescope. A planisphere is a star map which will help you to name the constellations you see. Dress warmly!

DO YOU KNOW

Distances in space are so great that they are measured in light-years. One light-year is 5,900 billion miles. This is the distance that light rays travel in a year.

Our sun (arrowed) is near the edge of the Milky Way, on a spiral arm 30,000 light-years from the center.

This is what the three main types of galaxy look like.

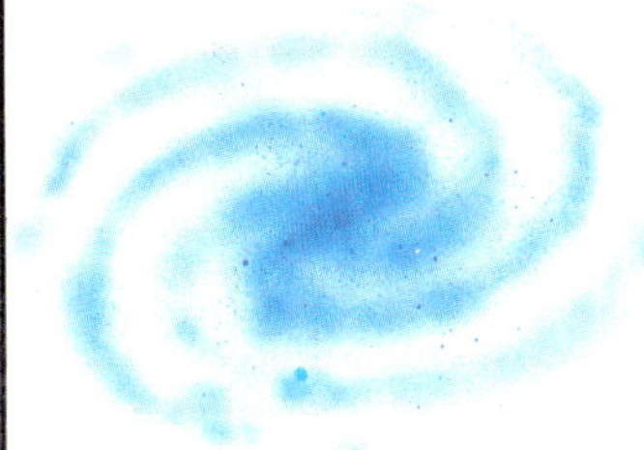

From above, spiral galaxies look like giant whirlpools, with long spiraling arms of stars. The nearest spiral galaxy to ours, the Andromeda Galaxy, is more than 2 million light-years away from Earth.

Elliptical galaxies are like spiral galaxies without arms. They are thought to be made up of old and dying stars.

Irregular galaxies can be any shape. They are all smaller than the Milky Way and seem to be made of young, newly formed stars.

What is the solar system?

Earth is one of nine planets which orbit the sun, and these planets and their moons make up the solar system – the word *solar* means "of the sun." The solar system also contains thousands of minor planets, called asteroids, and countless comets. The planets, asteroids, and comets are all held in their orbits by the sun's gravity, or pulling force.

DO YOU KNOW

Unlike stars, planets do not give off light. They shine at night because they reflect light from the sun.

The planets and other objects which orbit our sun travel in flattened circles called ellipses.

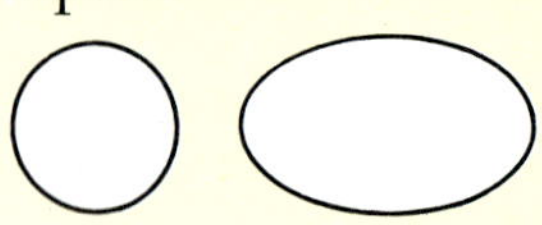

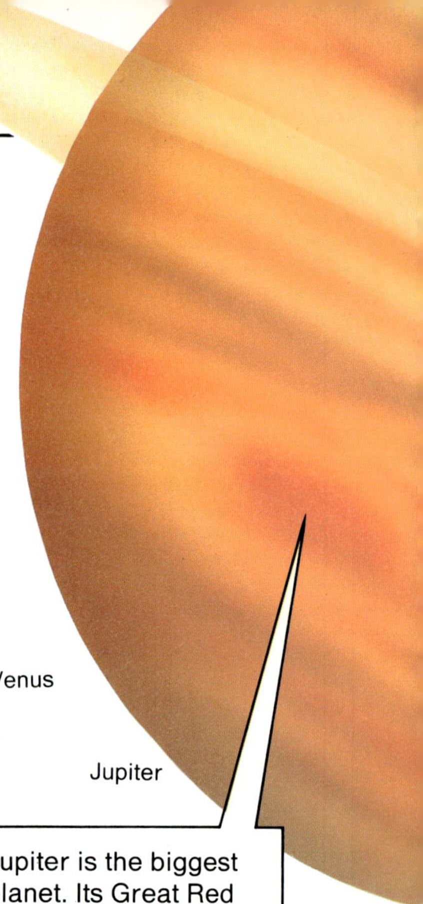

Jupiter is the biggest planet. Its Great Red Spot is a whirling cloud which is bigger than Earth.

Uranus, Jupiter, Neptune, and Saturn have rings. The rings are made of pieces of ice and dust.

PLANET FACTS

1 Mercury is the closest planet to the Sun.

2 Venus is hot, stormy, and covered in cloud.

3 Earth is the only planet in the solar system with air, oceans, and life.

4 Mars is a cold desert world.

About 50,000 asteroids form a belt between Mars and Jupiter.

5 Jupiter is the largest planet – all the rest could fit inside it.

6 Saturn has the brightest rings and the most moons (24 in all).

7 Uranus has 15 satellites and 13 rings.

8 The spacecraft Voyager 2 visited Neptune in 1989.

9 Pluto is the smallest of the planets and the least-known.

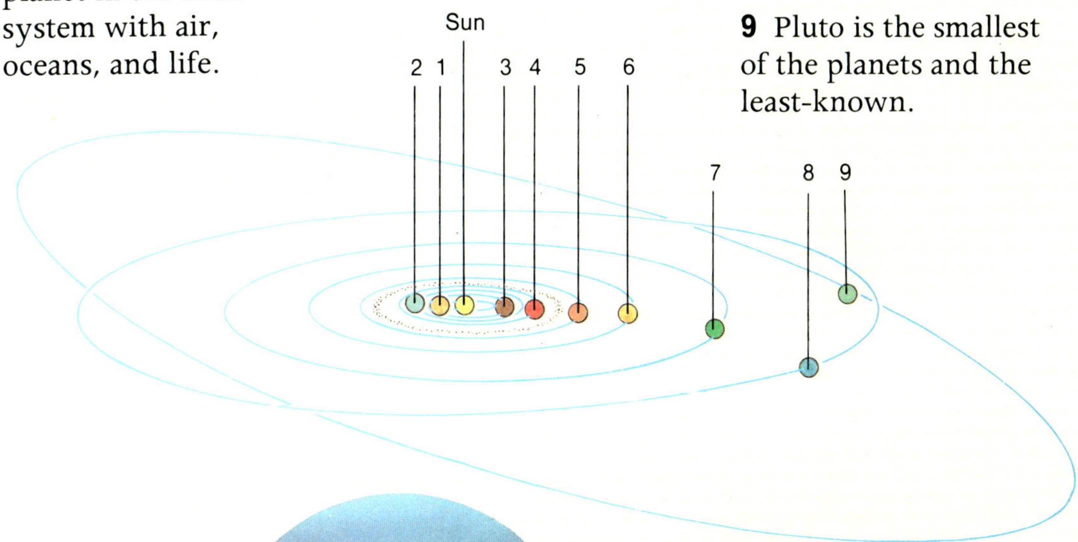

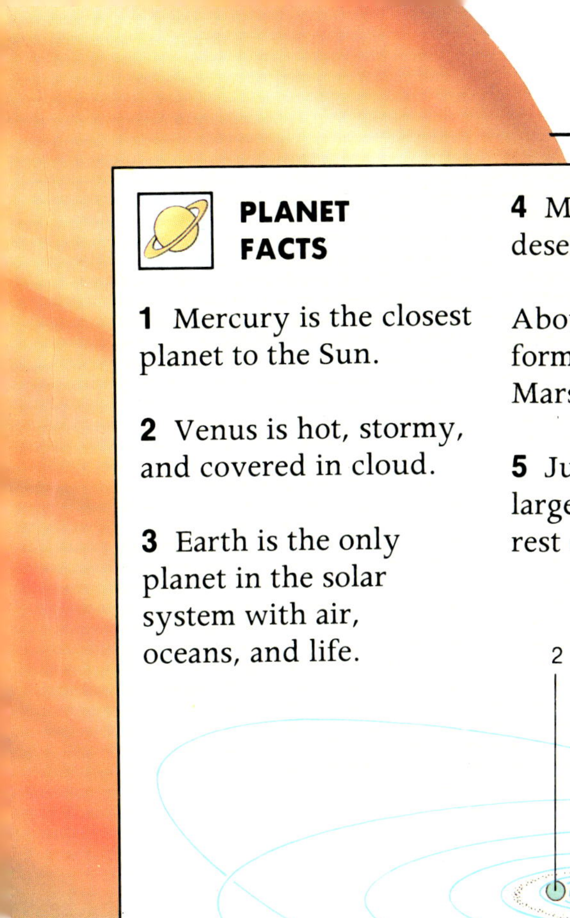

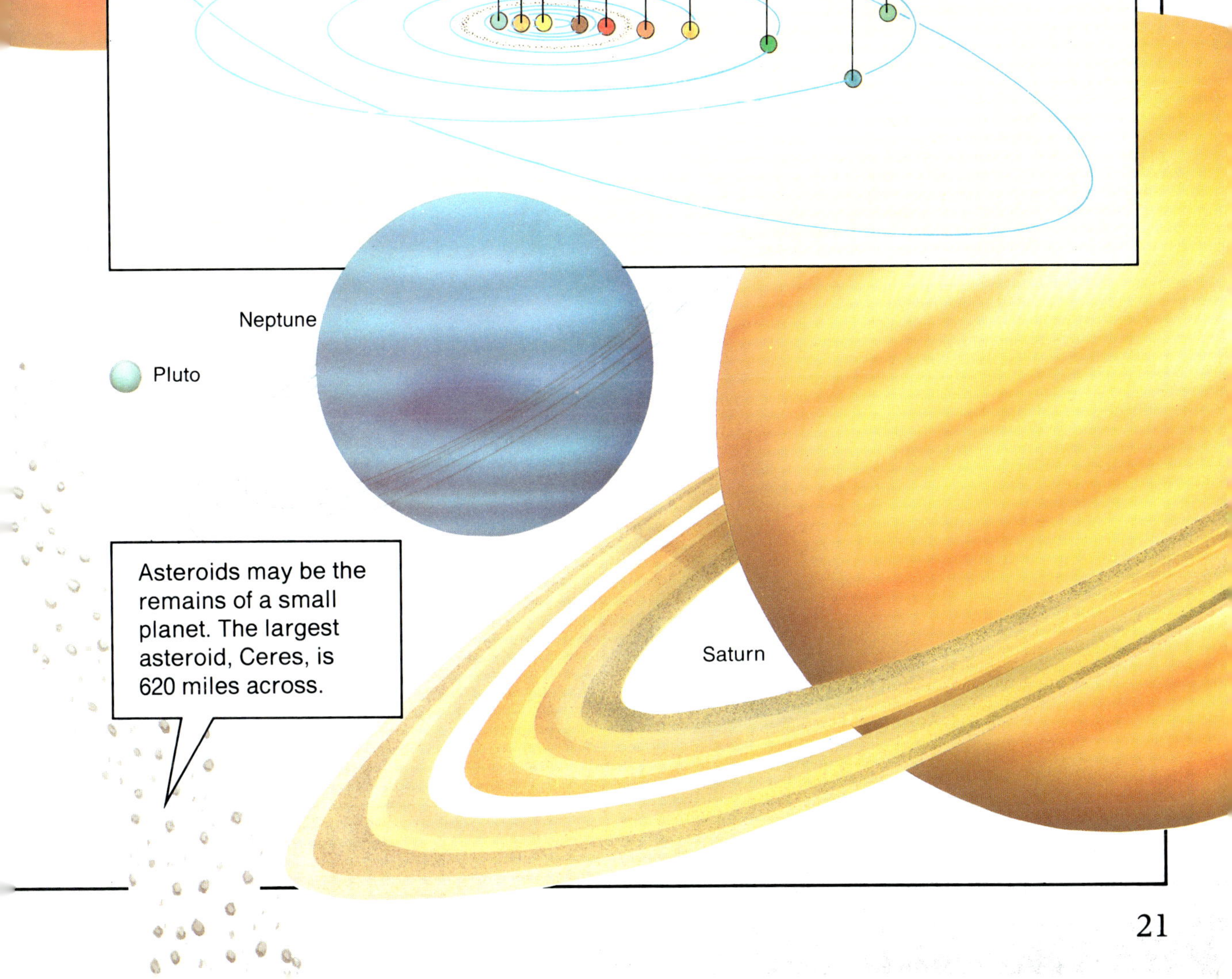

Asteroids may be the remains of a small planet. The largest asteroid, Ceres, is 620 miles across.

Which is the hottest planet?

The hottest planet is Venus, where the temperature reaches 896°F – almost five times as hot as boiling water! Venus is so hot because it is covered by thick heavy clouds of carbon dioxide gas, which trap the sun's heat like greenhouse glass.

VENUS FACTS

- 67 million miles from the sun
- 7,500 miles in diameter
- No moons
- Atmosphere – mainly carbon dioxide
- One day lasts 243 Earth days

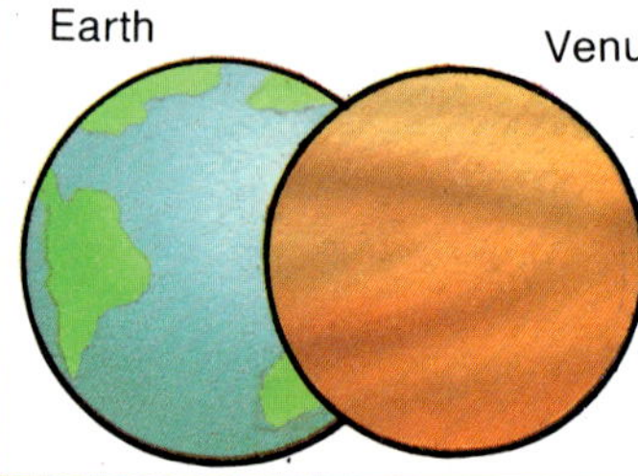

Which is the coldest planet?

Pluto is the coldest planet. It is so far from the sun that hardly any warmth reaches it. The temperature on Pluto is 369°F below freezing point. The lowest recorded temperature on Earth, just below -129°F, would seem like a heatwave on Pluto!

PLUTO FACTS

- 3.6 billion miles from the sun
- 1,500 miles in diameter
- One moon
- Atmosphere – not known
- One day lasts 6.4 Earth days

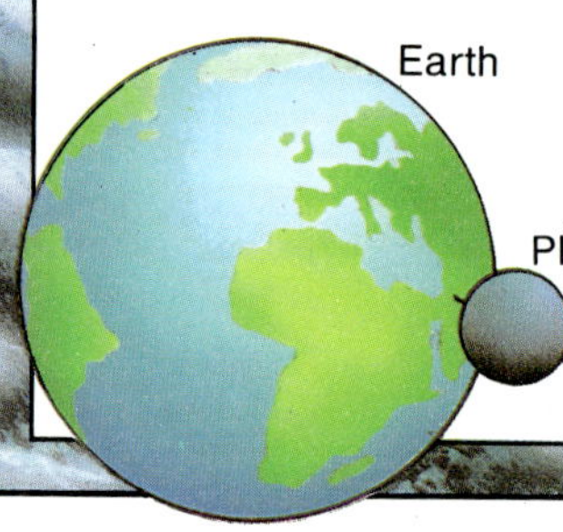

Which planet is nearest the sun?

Mercury is the nearest planet to the sun. At midday it is hotter than an oven – about 660°F. But at night it is freezing cold, because the planet has no atmosphere to keep the heat in.

The Mariner 10 spacecraft sent back the first pictures of Mercury in 1974–75.

MERCURY FACTS

- 36 million miles from the sun
- 3,032 miles in diameter
- No moons
- No atmosphere
- One day lasts 59 Earth days

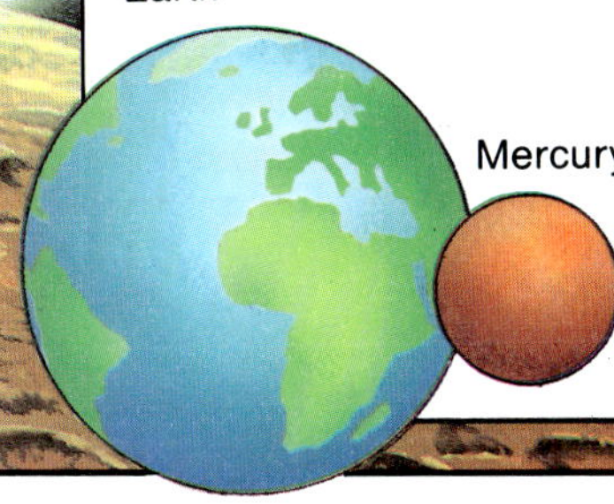

Which planet has the biggest moon?

The biggest planet, Jupiter, has the biggest moons in our solar system. It has 16 moons in all, and two of them are huge. Jupiter's largest moon is called Ganymede, and it is bigger than the planet Mercury. Another moon, Callisto, is nearly the same size.

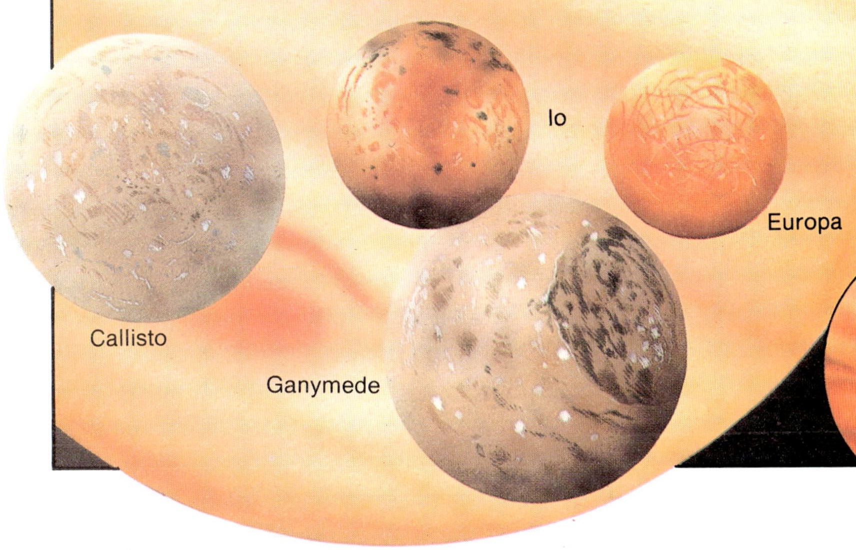

JUPITER FACTS

- 483 million miles from the sun
- 89,400 miles in diameter
- 16 moons
- Atmosphere – hydrogen and helium gases
- One day lasts nearly 10 Earth hours

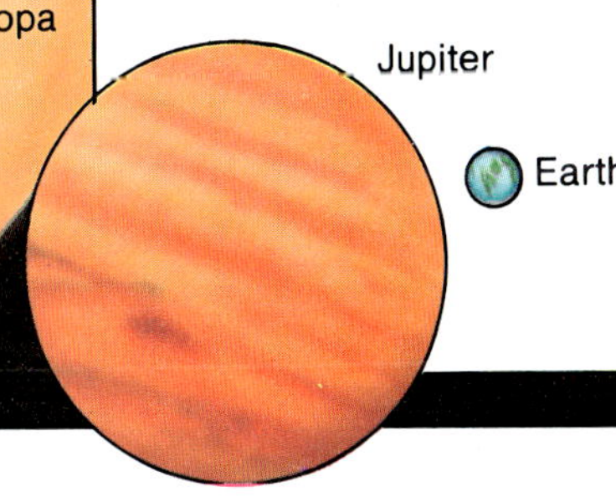

Is there life on Mars?

Mars is the fourth planet from the sun, and for a long time people wondered whether it was close enough to the sun to make some form of life possible. In 1976, two Viking spacecraft visited Mars, but they found no sign of life. Mars has very little air, no surface water, and it is bitterly cold – the temperature doesn't rise above the freezing point, even in summer. Mars may once have been warmer, however. If so, it may have had water and even, perhaps, simple forms of life.

MARS FACTS

- 142 million miles from the sun
- 4,223 miles in diameter
- 2 moons
- Atmosphere – carbon dioxide gas
- One day lasts about 24.5 Earth hours

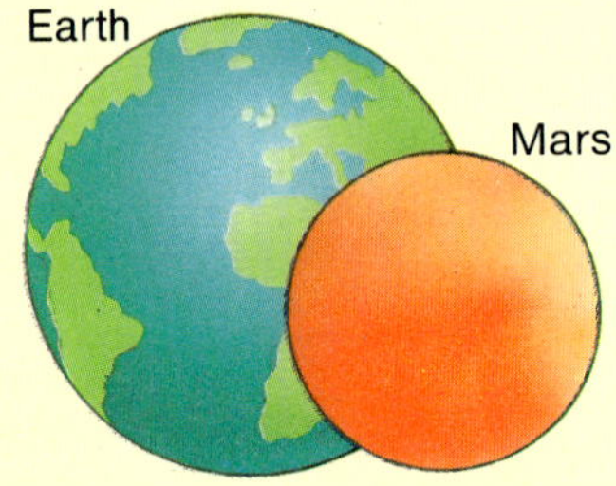

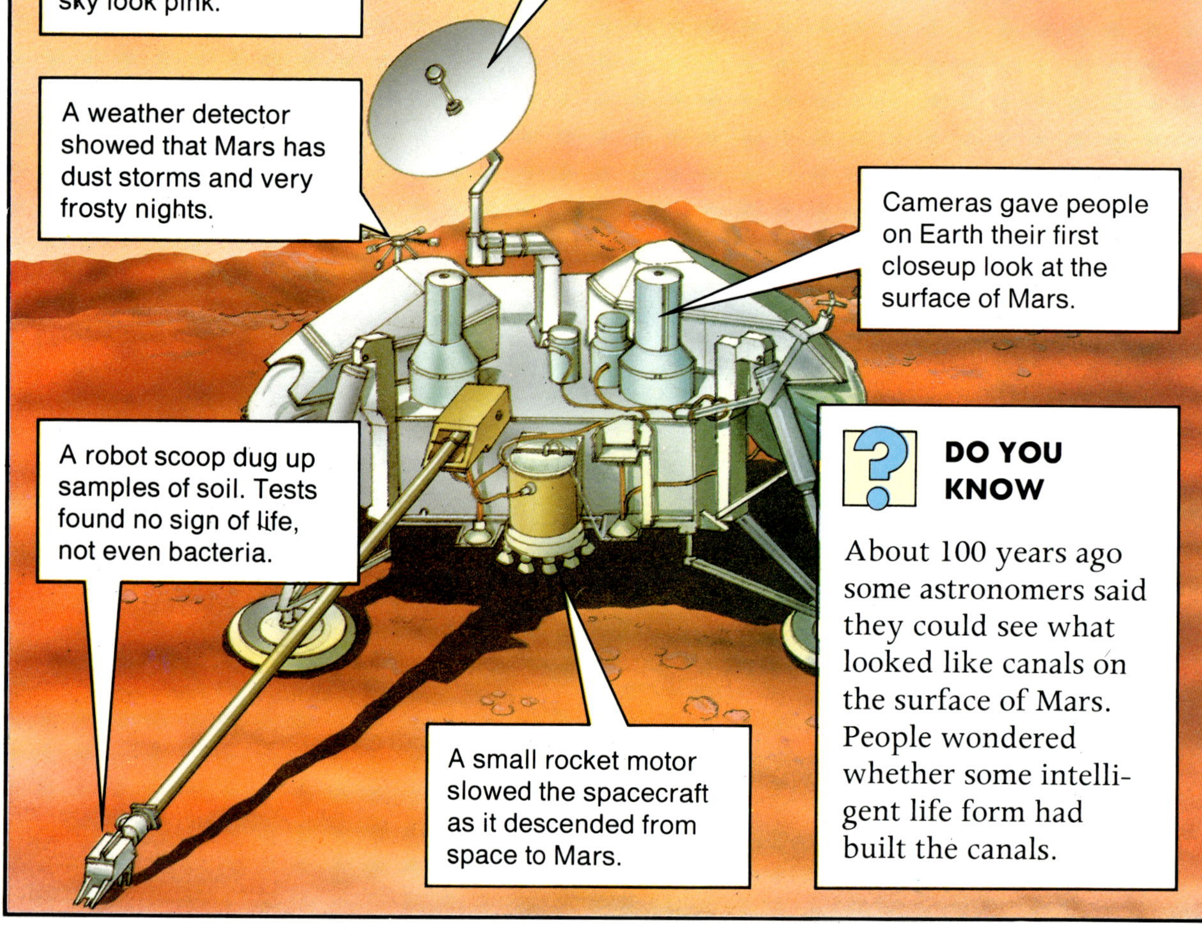

DO YOU KNOW

About 100 years ago some astronomers said they could see what looked like canals on the surface of Mars. People wondered whether some intelligent life form had built the canals.

What is Neptune like?

Until 1989, when the Voyager 2 spacecraft flew past Neptune, very little was known about this distant planet. We knew that it must be extremely cold, because it is so far from the sun. And astronomers had also spotted two moons. Voyager's cameras showed us a cold blue world, wrapped in storm clouds of methane gas – the blue is this gas, not oceans. Voyager also revealed that Neptune has six more moons, and that it has rings, like Saturn, Uranus, and Jupiter.

Neptune is covered by blue clouds of the gas methane. Voyager's cameras showed a giant storm cloud (below left), called the Great Dark Spot.

SPACE MESSAGES

Some spacecraft have carried messages on board, describing where they came from and who sent them. What kinds of things would you send into space to describe life on Earth – a newspaper, photographs, some music?

Voyager 2 left Earth in 1977. After visiting Neptune, it is continuing its journey out beyond the solar system.

NEPTUNE FACTS

- 2.8 billion miles from the sun
- 31,000 miles in diameter
- 8 moons
- Atmosphere – methane and other gases
- One day lasts about 16 Earth hours

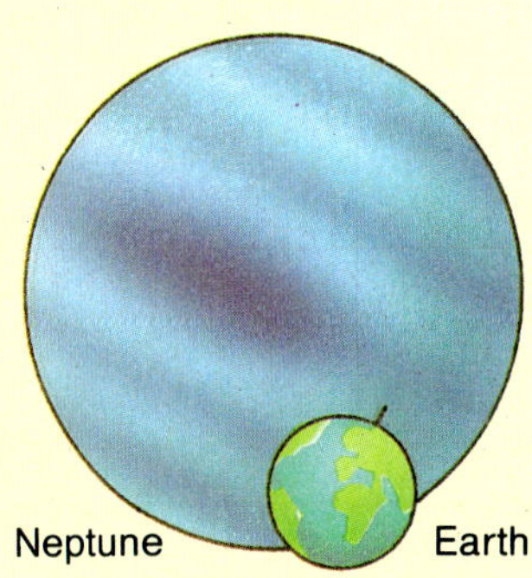

Who first landed on the moon?

In 1959, a Soviet spacecraft, Luna 2, crash-landed on the moon. Two years later, the United States began planning a spacecraft that could carry astronauts to the moon and back. By 1969 they were ready. Three astronauts traveled to the moon in the Apollo 11 spacecraft, which was launched from Earth by a giant Saturn rocket. The main spacecraft orbited the moon, while astronauts Neil Armstrong and Edwin Aldrin flew down in a small landing craft. They set foot on the moon on July 20, 1969.

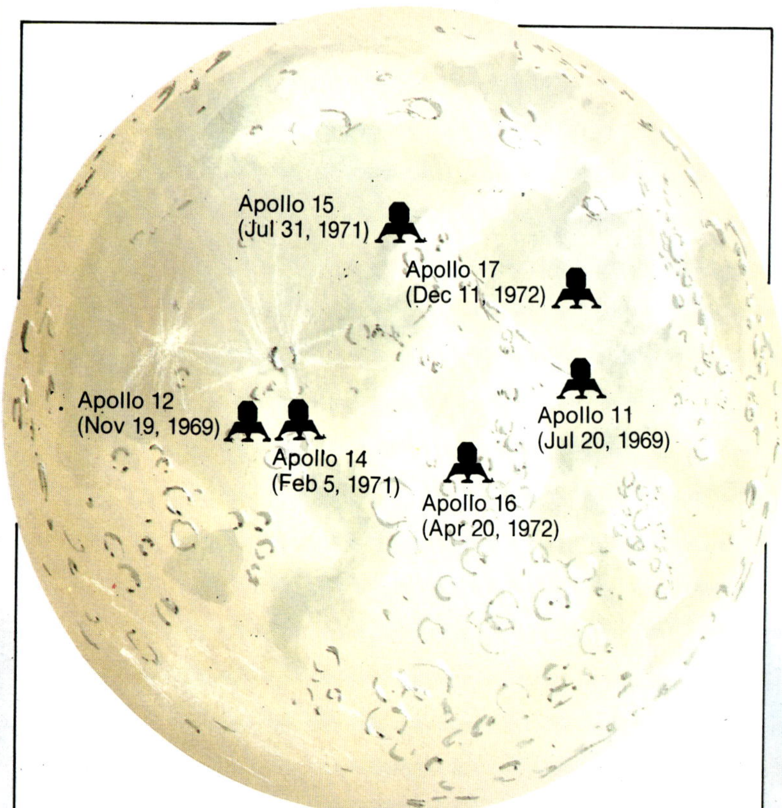

Between 1969 and 1972, six Apollo spacecraft landed on the moon, and 12 astronauts explored different parts of its surface. The longest visit was in December 1972, when Apollo 17 astronauts Eugene Cernan and Harrison Schmitt stayed for almost 75 hours.

MOON FACTS

- 238,000 miles from Earth
- 2,160 miles in diameter
- Atmosphere – none
- One day lasts 27.3 Earth days
- It can be as hot as 260°F and as cold as -280°F.
- It is roughly as wide as Australia.

HOW FAR IS THE MOON?

1 To get an idea of the size of the moon in comparison to Earth, use a small marble and a golf ball.

2 The diameter of the golf ball is roughly 1.5 inches. Cut a piece of string 30 times as long.

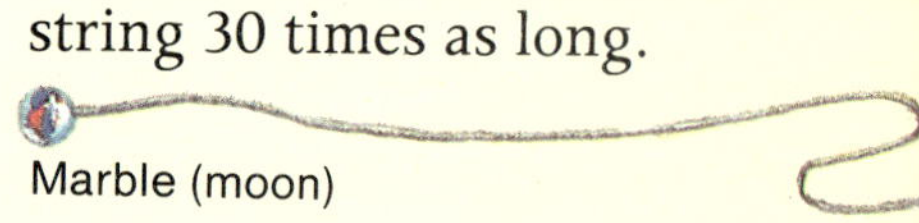

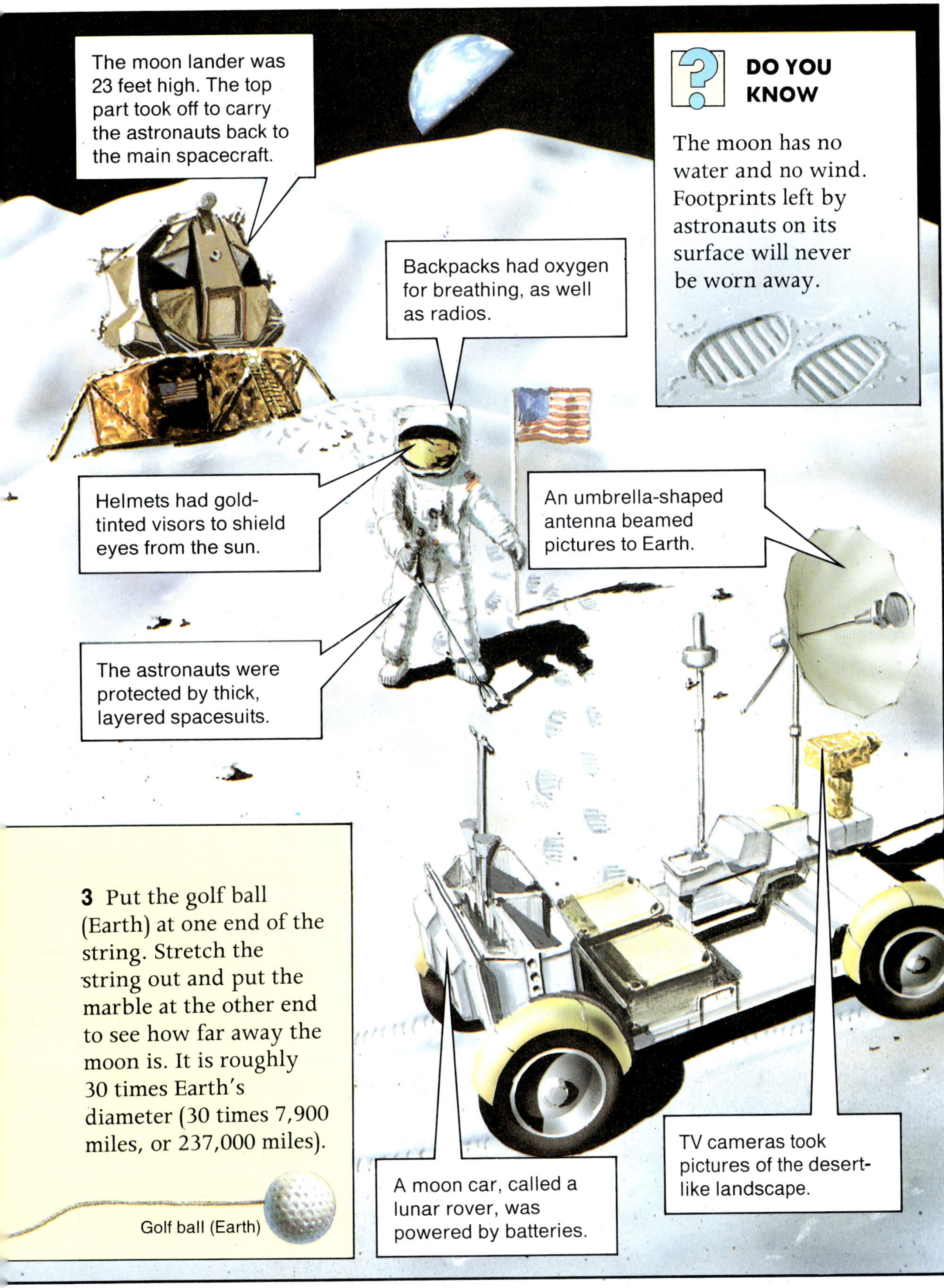

DO YOU KNOW

The moon has no water and no wind. Footprints left by astronauts on its surface will never be worn away.

3 Put the golf ball (Earth) at one end of the string. Stretch the string out and put the marble at the other end to see how far away the moon is. It is roughly 30 times Earth's diameter (30 times 7,900 miles, or 237,000 miles).

Why does the moon change shape?

From Earth, we can see only one face or side of the moon. It appears to change shape because we see this face from different angles during the $29\frac{1}{2}$ days the moon takes to orbit Earth. The moon is lit by the sun; it doesn't give off any light of its own. But the sun lights only one half of the moon at a time, leaving the other half dark and invisible. Sometimes the sun lights the entire face of the moon that we see from Earth. At other times only part is sunlit.

DO YOU KNOW

The moon spins once on its axis each time it goes around Earth. This is why we just see one face of the moon. Only space travelers have seen the other, far side of the moon.

If you look at the Moon each night for a month, you'll see it change shape in the way shown below.

The word *gibbous* means "humpbacked."

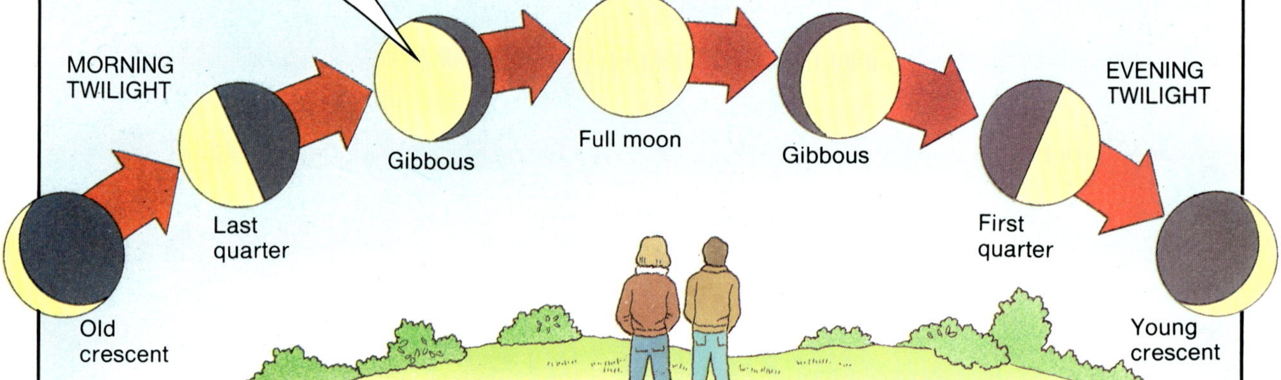

MAKE A MOON SPINNER

The moon is held in its orbit by Earth's gravity, or pulling power. Without this, the moon would fly off into space. Here's a way to see how gravity acts.

1 Tie a length of string to a small plastic bucket. Make sure your knots are strong and that you have plenty of open space around you.

2 Whirl the bucket around. You'll feel a force tugging it outward – only the string stops the bucket from flying off. Earth's gravity is like the piece of string, holding the moon in its orbit.

Why do eclipses happen?

There are two types of eclipse, and they happen for different reasons. An eclipse of the sun takes place if the moon passes in front of the sun. Sometimes the moon blocks out the sun completely and for a short time day becomes night. This is called a total eclipse. There are also eclipses of the moon. These happen if the full moon passes through Earth's shadow.

NEVER LOOK AT THE SUN

Never look directly at the sun during an eclipse. It is just as dangerous to your eyes at these times as when it is shining normally.

During a total eclipse of the sun, only its brilliant corona flares around it.

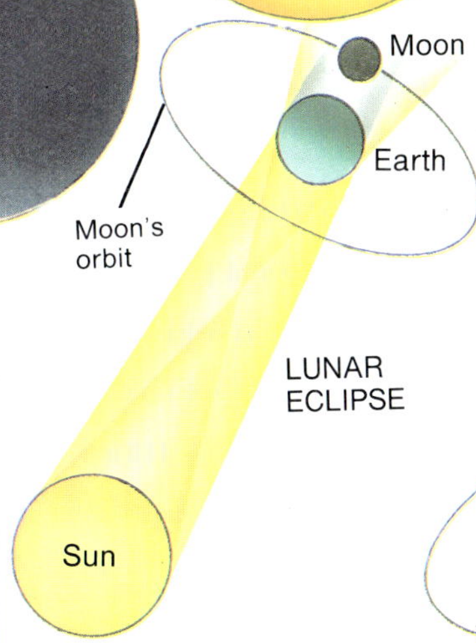

An eclipse of the moon (left) happens when it passes through Earth's shadow. The moon doesn't disappear, because this shadow isn't completely black. Enough dim sunlight gets through to turn the moon a reddish brown color. A total eclipse can last for over $1\frac{1}{2}$ hours.

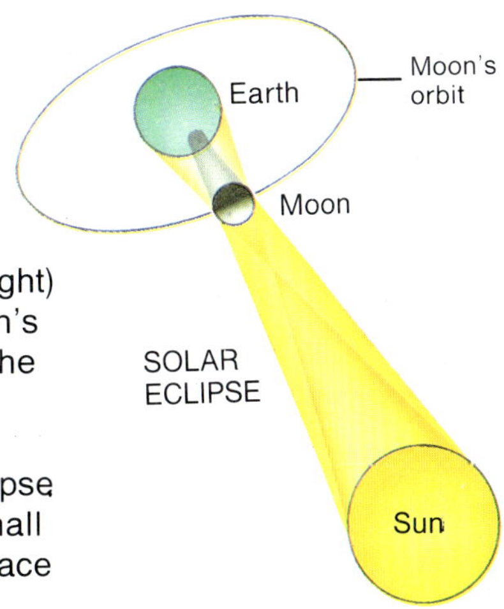

An eclipse of the sun (right) happens when the moon's orbit brings it between the sun and Earth. Solar eclipses occur at least twice a year; a total eclipse is only seen inside a small area on the Earth's surface and lasts just a few minutes.

Eclipses must have been very frightening before people knew why they happen. In the East, people believed eclipses were caused by a dragon trying to eat the sun or the moon.

When did the space age begin?

The space age began on October 4, 1957, when the USSR launched Sputnik 1, the world's first artificial satellite. The first space flight by a person was on April 12, 1961. Yuri Gagarin, a Soviet cosmonaut, orbited Earth once in the Vostok 1 spacecraft, proving that people could travel safely into space and back again.

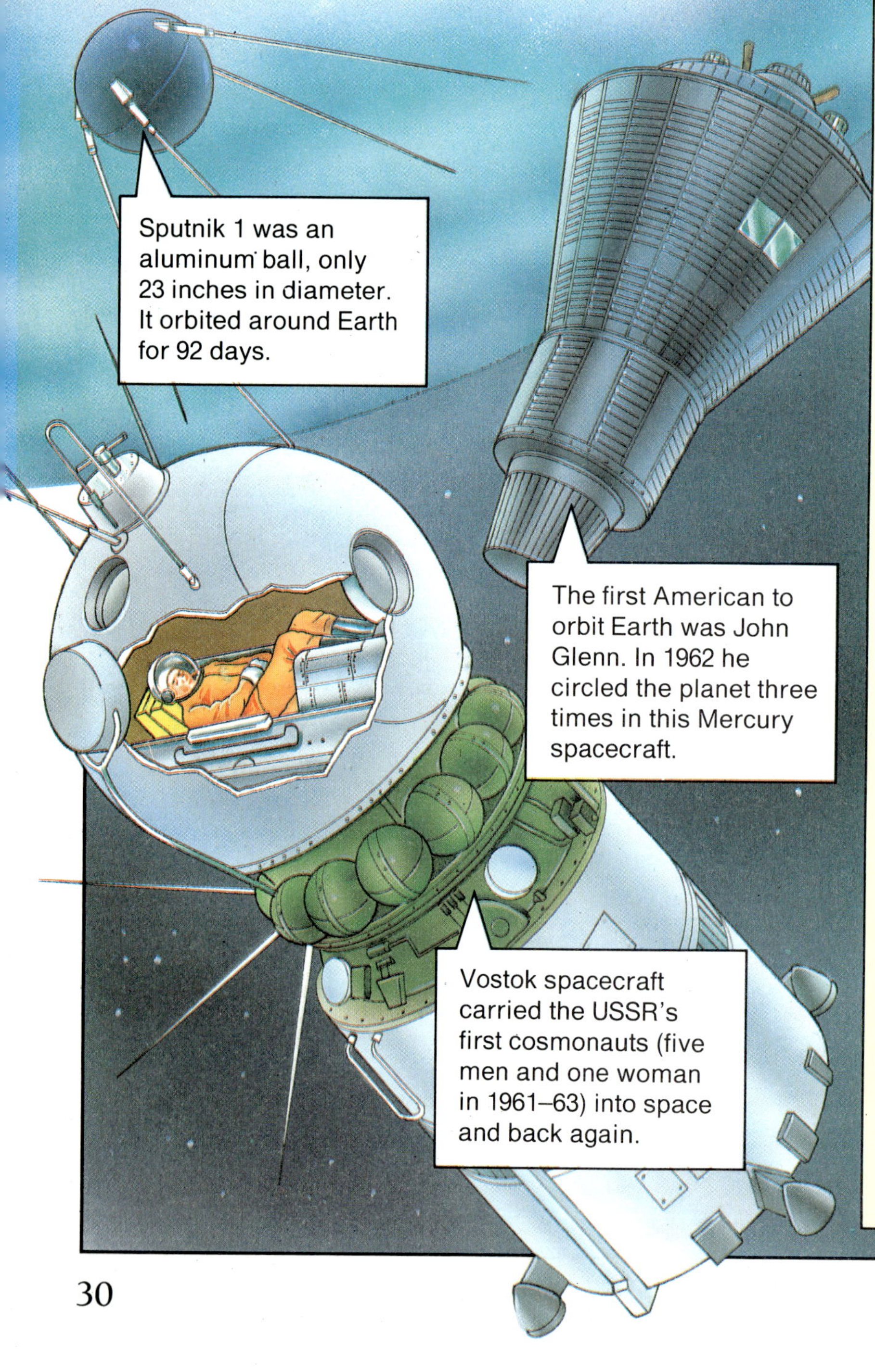

SPACE FACTS

- The first animal in space was a dog called Laika. Laika was launched in 1957, in the USSR's Sputnik 2.
- The first TV pictures to be beamed across the Atlantic Ocean via satellite were relayed by Telstar (US).
- The first closeup pictures of the planet Mars were sent back to Earth in 1965, by the US spacecraft Mariner 4.
- The first spacecraft to fly around the moon and land back on Earth was the USSR's Zond 5, in 1968.
- The first spacecraft to land on Mars were two US Viking probes (July and September 1976).
- The first spacecraft to visit the outer planets of the solar system was the US Voyager 2. It was launched in 1977 and flew past the planet Neptune in 1989.

When were space rockets invented?

The first space rockets were invented in the 1950s, but the Soviet scientist Konstantin Tsiolkovski (1857-1935) had realized how they would work much earlier. People began to test small rockets in the 1920s, and during World War II (1939-45) the Germans invented the V2 rocket, which was used as a weapon. After the war, scientists improved the V2's design until they made rockets powerful enough to travel into space.

DO YOU KNOW

Gunpowder firework rockets were invented in China, but no one knows when. They were known in Europe by the year 1241.

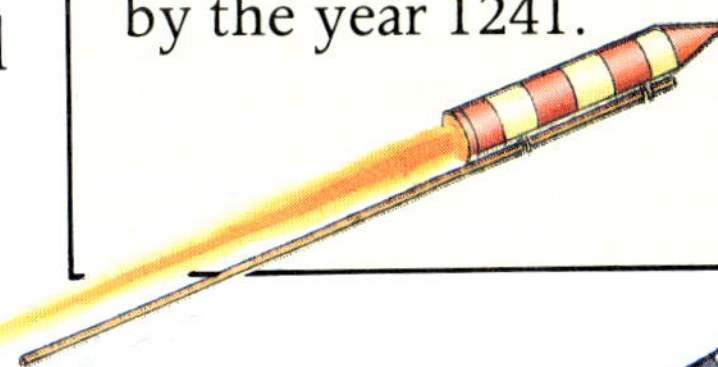

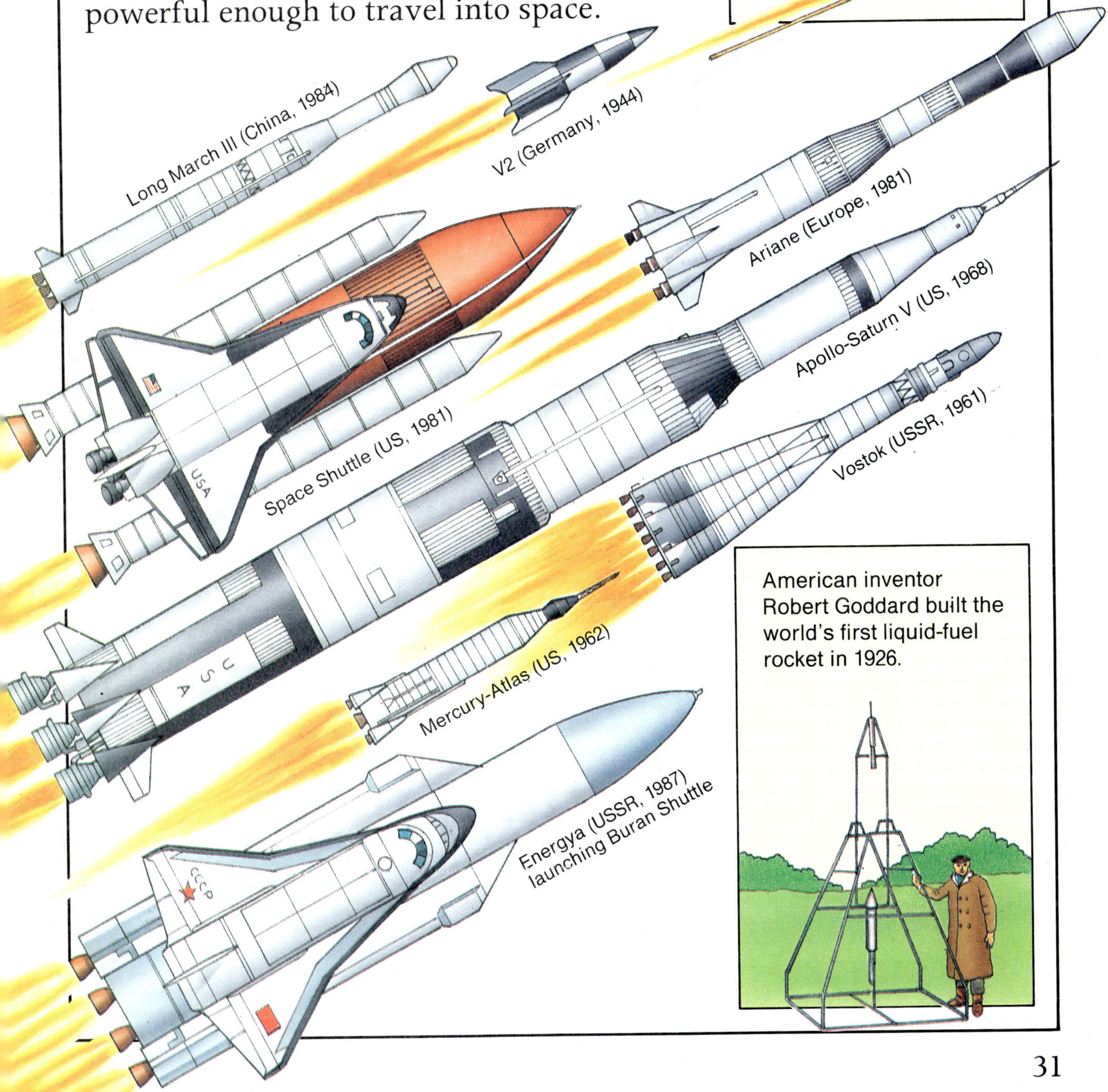

American inventor Robert Goddard built the world's first liquid-fuel rocket in 1926.

Who made the first spacewalk?

The Soviet cosmonaut Alexei Leonov made the first spacewalk, on March 18, 1965. Leonov left the Voskhod 2 spacecraft and stayed outside for 24 minutes. A safety line made sure he didn't float away.

Since that time Soviet cosmonauts and American astronauts have spent hours working outside their spacecrafts. They have even been able to repair their spacecraft while on spacewalks.

DO YOU KNOW

The USA's John Young went into space six times between 1965 and 1983. In 1981, he commanded the first flight of the shuttle Columbia.

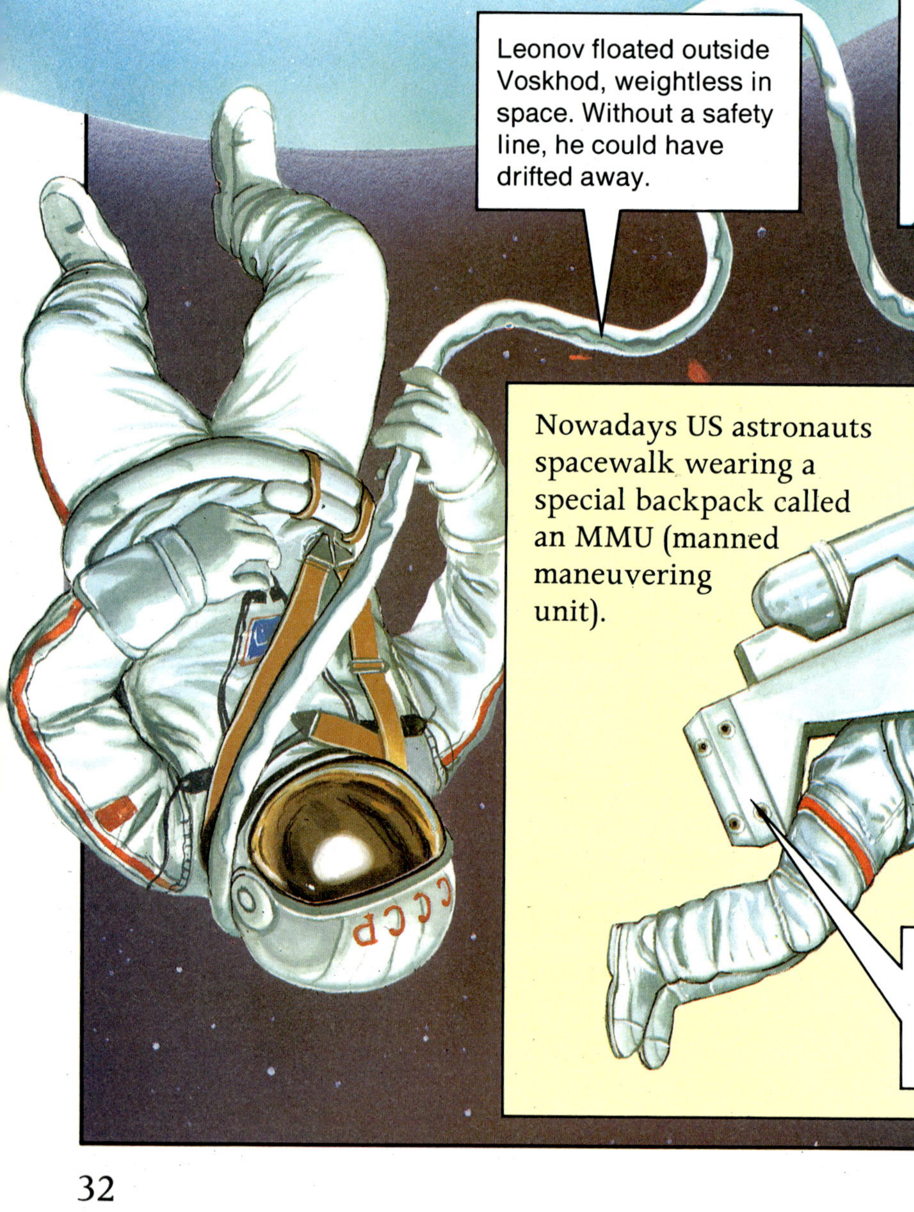

Nowadays US astronauts spacewalk wearing a special backpack called an MMU (manned maneuvering unit).

Who was the first woman in space?

The first spacewoman was Valentina Tereshkova of the USSR. She began training to be a cosmonaut in 1962, and on June 16, 1963, she was launched into space in the spacecraft Vostok 6. She then spent more than two days orbiting Earth.

DO YOU KNOW

The crews of the USA's Apollo and USSR's Soyuz spacecraft met up in space in 1975.

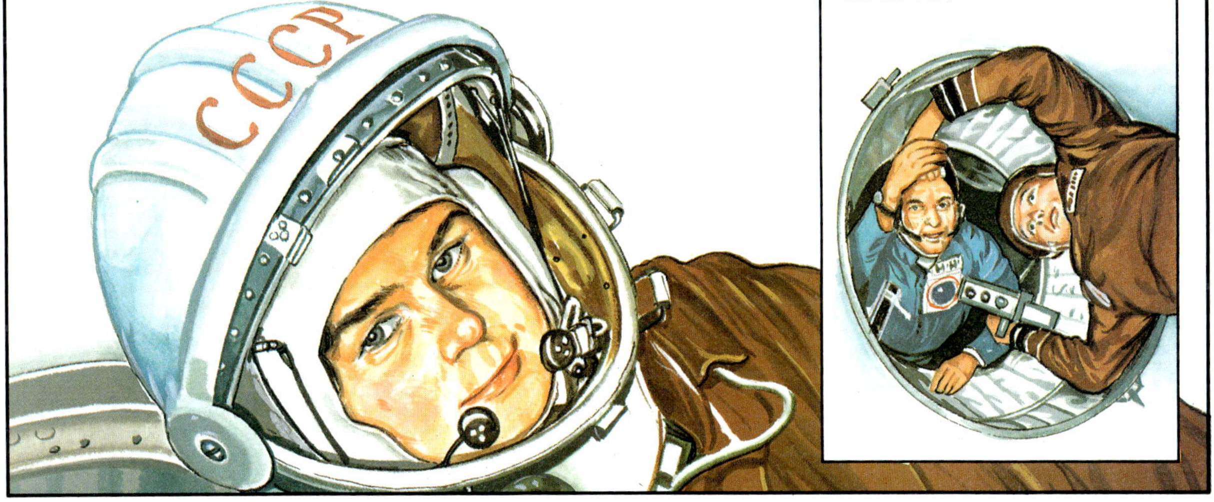

How long can people stay in space?

Soviet cosmonauts have lived for as long as a year on board space stations orbiting Earth. Doctors study the effects of these long space flights on the cosmonauts' bodies, to make sure they stay fit and well.

What is living in space like?

Although today's space stations are not as big as the futuristic one shown here, life on board is still fairly comfortable. The biggest difference from living on Earth is that there is no gravity in space. Without this force to hold things down, everything floats. This makes washing and eating a little tricky! Space travelers have to hold on to something or strap themselves down so they don't float around.

Because there is no gravity at all in space, washing is difficult – water floats there, just like everything else does. Space travelers have special showers in which the water is vacuumed away so that no droplets can escape.

Space stations will be powered by solar panels, which collect the sun's light and turn it into electricity.

Because of the special conditions in space, scientists can do experiments that are impossible on Earth. They can make new alloys (mixtures of metals) and medicines. They also study how plants grow when gravity is low, and whether animals like fish and spiders behave differently in space.

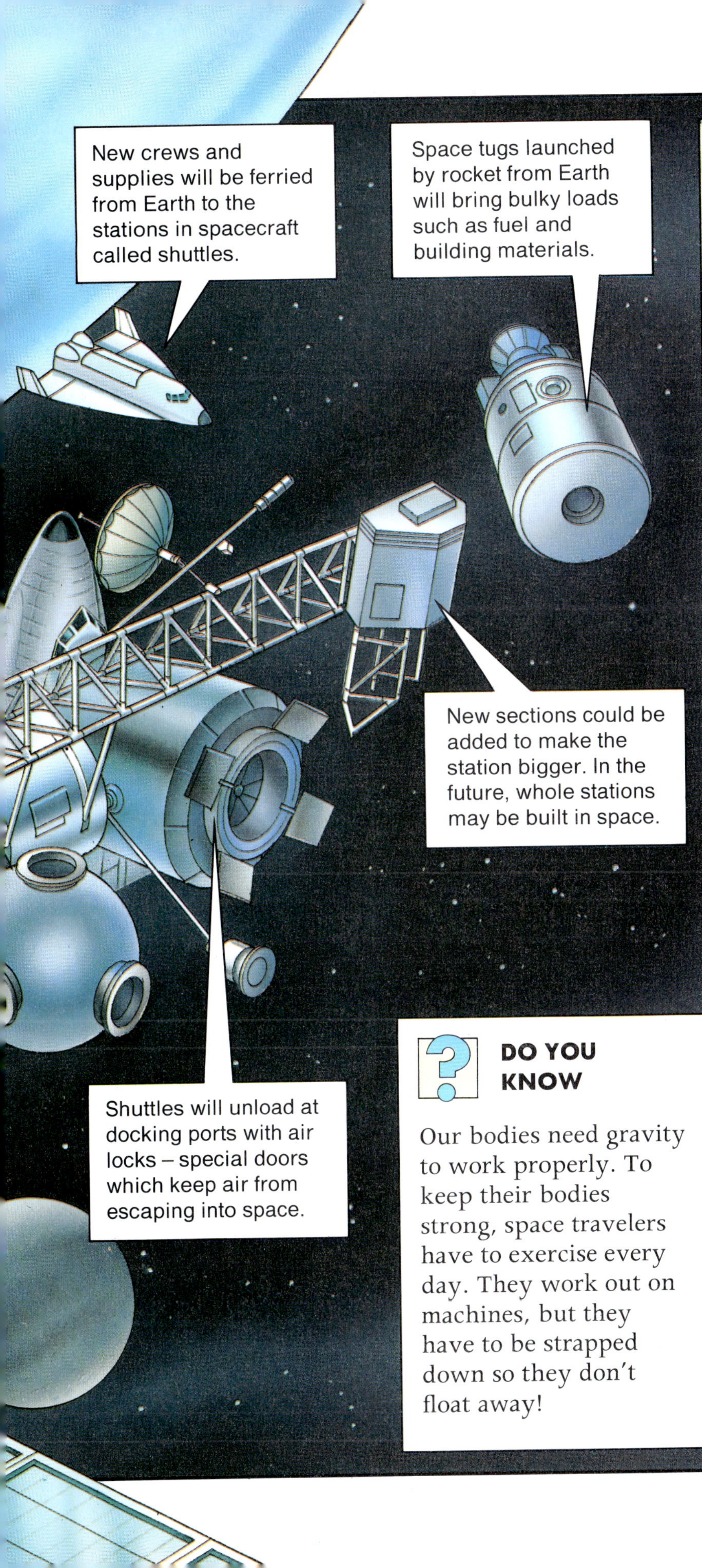

SPACE TRAVEL FACTS

- To date, about 200 people have traveled into space. Most have been scientists or pilots.
- The most dangerous times for space travelers are during the spacecraft's takeoff from Earth and its reentry into the atmosphere.
- Astronauts and cosmonauts spend years training on Earth before they travel into space. To help them get used to weightlessness, they wear spacesuits and practice working while floating in a deep tank of water.

DO YOU KNOW

Our bodies need gravity to work properly. To keep their bodies strong, space travelers have to exercise every day. They work out on machines, but they have to be strapped down so they don't float away!

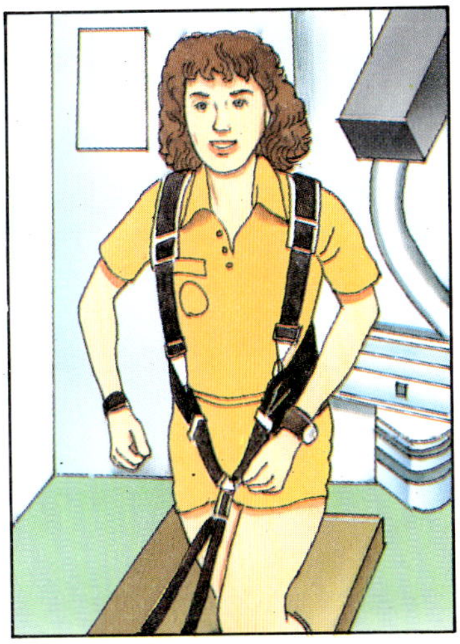

How did the universe begin?

Nobody knows just how the universe began, but we know that it is changing. The millions of galaxies in the universe seem to be speeding farther and farther apart – as though the universe is expanding, or getting bigger. Because of this, many scientists think that at one time all the matter, or material, in the universe was close together, and that a vast explosion sent it flying apart. Scientists call this explosion the big bang.

DO YOU KNOW

Quasars are the most distant objects that we know of in the universe. They are huge, bright galaxies very far away. The most distant known quasar is hurtling away at almost the speed of light – which is 186,000 miles a second! It is at least 6 billion light-years away, which means that the light now reaching Earth from this quasar began its journey toward us before the solar system existed!

BALLOON UNIVERSE

1 Paint galaxy shapes close together all over a large balloon.

2 Let the paint dry, then blow up the balloon to see how the galaxies are moving apart as the universe expands.

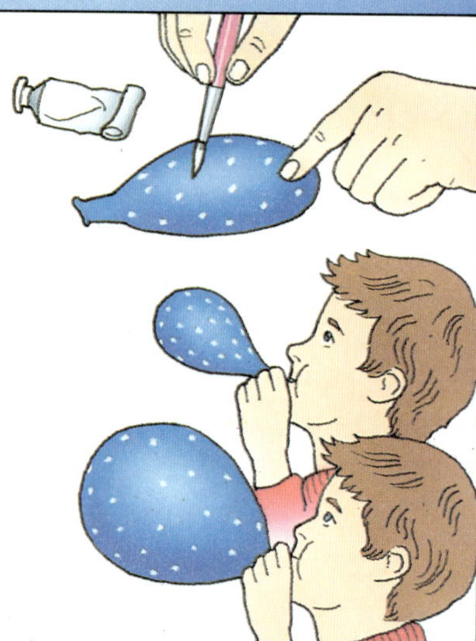

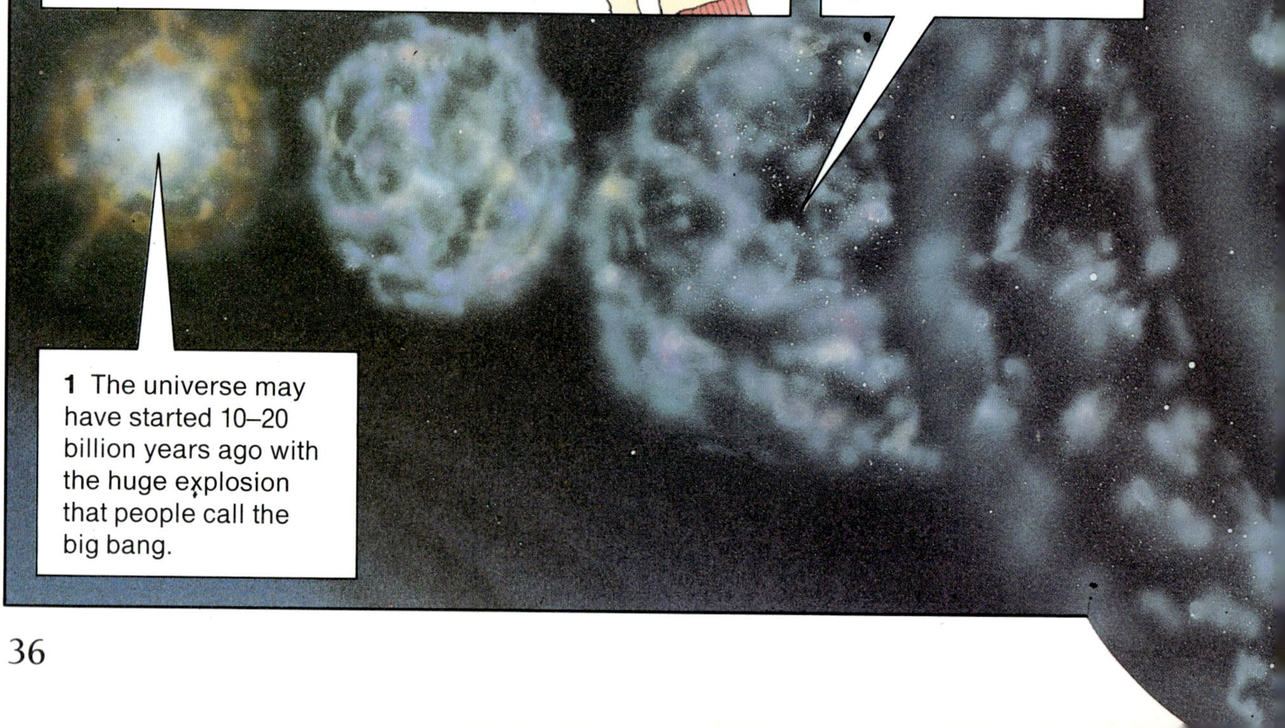

2 About 1 billion years after the big bang, the first stars formed inside the developing galaxies.

1 The universe may have started 10–20 billion years ago with the huge explosion that people call the big bang.

We live on a tiny planet close to a medium-size star (the sun), in one of millions of galaxies.

SATURN FACTS

- 886 million miles from the sun
- 74,980 miles in diameter
- 24 moons
- Atmosphere – hydrogen and helium gases
- One day lasts about 10.8 Earth hours

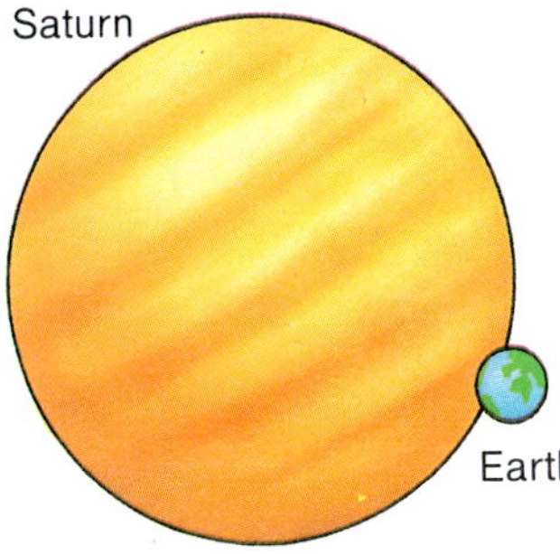

3 The universe is still expanding as the galaxies keep on speeding apart. The universe has no edge – there is always more space ahead.

Will the universe ever end?

Until we know more about how the universe began, we can only guess whether it will ever end. If it did start with the big bang, the force of the explosion may be strong enough to keep the galaxies flying through space forever. Then the universe will never end. However, some scientists think that the galaxies might go into reverse and come closer together. Eventually they will crash into each other, and the universe will end in a big crunch.

URANUS FACTS

- 1.8 billion miles from the sun
- 32,490 miles in diameter
- 15 moons
- Atmosphere – hydrogen, helium, and methane gases
- One day lasts about 17 Earth hours

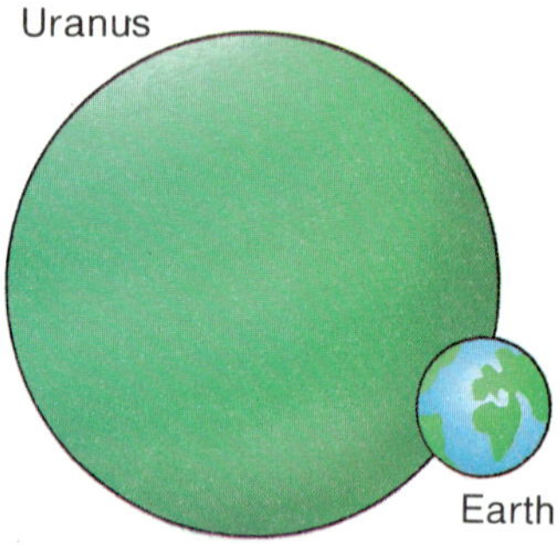

1 Billions of years in the future, there may come a time when the galaxies' flight through space slows down.

2 The galaxies would stop expanding and go into reverse. The universe would then begin to shrink.

3 All the matter, or material, in the universe may be squashed together in a big crunch.

Useful words

Asteroid There are thousands of these mini-planets orbiting the sun. Even the largest is much smaller than the moon.

Astronomer Someone who studies the stars.

Atmosphere The layer of gases around a planet. Earth's atmosphere is mainly nitrogen and oxygen gas. Mars and Venus have mainly carbon dioxide.

Axis An imaginary line through the center of a planet. A planet spins on its axis.

Billion One thousand million (1,000,000,000).

Comet A huge cloud of gas and dust which orbits the sun.

Constellation A group of bright stars which make a pattern in the sky.

Core The center of a star or a planet.

Corona The outermost layer of the sun. It looks like a faint halo and stretches millions of miles into space.

Cosmonaut The Russian word for a space traveler.

Galaxy A huge group of stars – even a small galaxy may contain several million stars. There are millions of galaxies in the universe.

Gravity Every object in the universe has this pulling force. Earth's gravity keeps our feet on the ground and stops us from floating up into the air. The sun's much stronger gravity keeps Earth in its orbit and stops it from flying off into space.

Light-year The distance a ray of light travels through space in one year – about 5,900 billion miles. Distances in space are measured in light-years.

Orbit The curved path of something that travels around a star or a planet. Each planet, including Earth, has its own orbit around the sun.

Satellite Anything that orbits a planet. Moons are natural satellites. A spacecraft orbiting a planet is an artificial, or man-made, satellite.

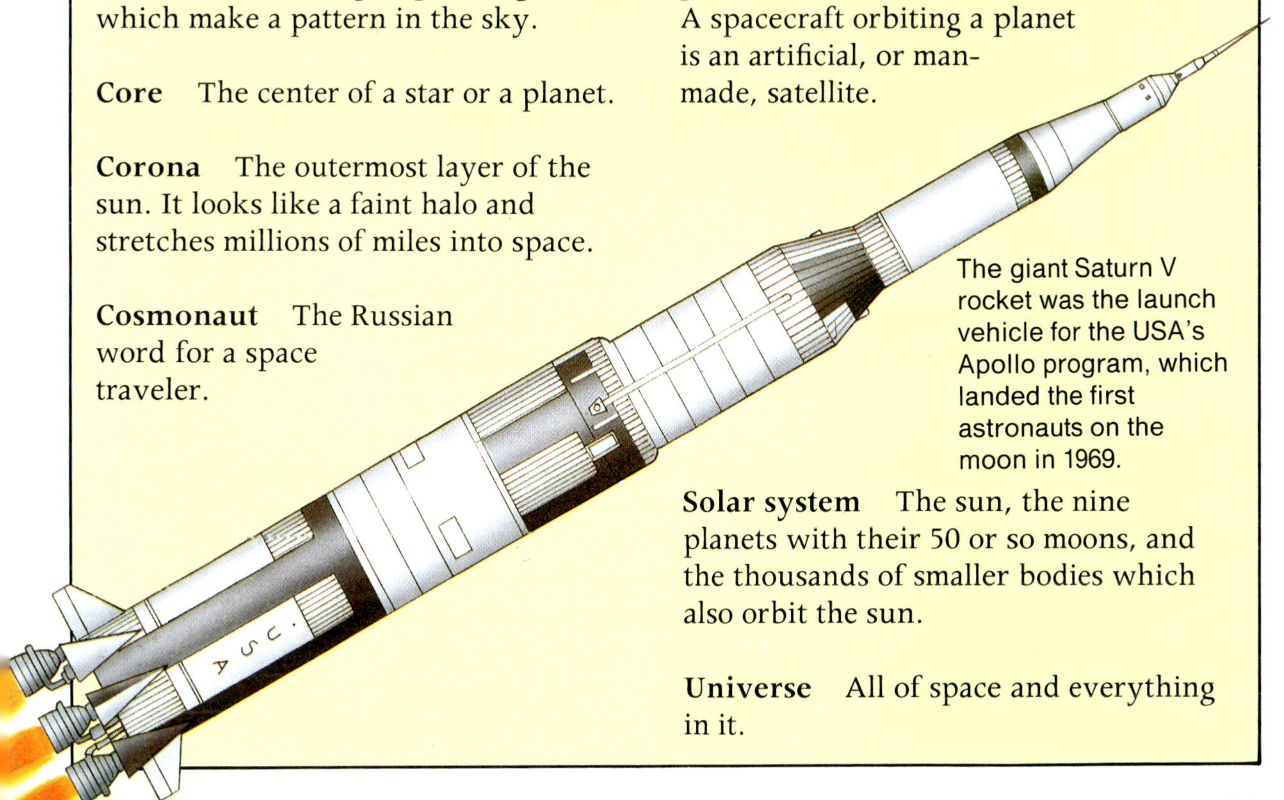

The giant Saturn V rocket was the launch vehicle for the USA's Apollo program, which landed the first astronauts on the moon in 1969.

Solar system The sun, the nine planets with their 50 or so moons, and the thousands of smaller bodies which also orbit the sun.

Universe All of space and everything in it.

Index